Betty Lou

STEVEN PHILLIPS

BETTY LOU

ISBN: 9781093761009

CONTENTS

PREFACE

I am Betty Lou's eldest son. I'm the Stevie you will read about in this story. Mom considered her early years to be among the happiest of her life; growing up on a farm in southern Indiana, meeting and marrying her first love, and migrating west on fabled Route 66 with two other colorful families. It was always Mom's wish that her story of the early years be told. Mom called me one day in her later years: she asked that I write the story. We spent hours going through old black and white photos. We had a great time recounting memories from those free-wheeling years; we laughed a lot and I learned a lot about Mom's life before I came along.

I had the experience of living, for one year, nearly the same rural Indiana life that Mom had lived. At the age of five, I moved in with Grandpa and Grandma to attend my first year of school in Paris Crossing. I slept in the same bedroom on the same feather mattress. I knew the terror of the steam locomotives that thundered by the house in the night. I went to the same country school where Mom had graduated in 1945. This gave me a frame of reference that brought her earliest memories to life. *Betty Lou* is told through my mother's eyes. Mom passed away on July 23, 2016 at the age of eighty-nine. This is her remarkable story.

BETTY LOU

1 PARIS CROSSING

I was born on a small farm near the town of Paris Crossing, Indiana in 1927. Paris Crossing was typical of the rural farming communities that dotted the landscape of southern Indiana. We had a general store, schoolhouse, Baptist church, post office, and an auto garage with a single gas pump. There was an assortment of modest homes, and one imposing multi-story brick mansion on tree-lined Main Street. The villages of Commiskey and Lovett were our neighbors to the north, and Deputy, the largest of the little farm towns, our neighbor to the south.

Farming had been the way of life here for generations. Nearly all of the farmers grew enough produce to sustain the family, with some left over to sell or trade locally. Everyone kept chickens, and at least one milk cow. The larger farms had draft horses for plowing and transport. We didn't keep pigs, but many of our neighbors did.

My first childhood memories are from the early years of The Great Depression. Front page stories in the newspaper reported fortunes being lost overnight. Images of unemployed men lined up at city soup kitchens illustrated the depth and extent of the financial collapse. Nothing really changed in our little corner of the world. The great national prosperity of the 1920's had also passed us by. Money just didn't play a big part in our lives. We had very little, but we needed little more than what we had. The four-room farm house I grew up in was heated by a black potbelly stove that burned wood and coal which lay abundant everywhere. Our night light came from kerosene lamps. Water, cold, clear and delicious, came from a spring that exited at the bottom of the hill behind the barn. In the barn were two cows that faithfully provided milk that Mom made into butter, and cream. Nearby, a big chicken coop housed a great flock of hens that provided fresh eggs, and occasionally a main course of Mom's secret recipe fried chicken.

I was the baby of the family. Sister Florence was the oldest, followed by Genevieve, Jay, Alice, and me. By the time I came into the world, Florence and Ginny had married and moved to the city. Big brother Jay was around twelve years old; Alice was four or five.

I'm sure Mom and Dad loved us all equally, but Jay was the answer to prayers for a Cook son, and was always special in their eyes. If there was any favoritism, Jay was oblivious to it. He had assumed all the chores my older sisters used to do, and then some. Water had to be brought up from the spring every day by bucket, often requiring several trips carrying two heavy buckets at a time. There was no trash pickup; all refuse was piled in a heap in a clearing above the spring. When the trash heap reached a certain size, it was set ablaze.

Our perishable food was stored in an icebox. In warmer months, the large blocks of ice melted quickly, and needed to be replaced. Jay brought the new blocks from the ice house in Humphrey's Cash Store home in a pull wagon. Jay had a pet goose named Matilda. She would tag along on the walks to the store like an overgrown puppy. Jay's help was a blessing for Daddy, who experienced occasional shortness of breath and chest pains. His ability to do physical work had been in decline for years due to a chronic heart condition.

Betty Lou and Big Sister Alice 1929

Just outside our kitchen door was a blood-stained tree stump. Two large nails were driven into the flat surface of the stump. Wedged into a crevice on the stump was a hand axe. Mom would go to the coop with an apron full of chicken feed as she did every day. If it was Sunday, or if we were expecting company, the first unfortunate chicken to wander within reach was promptly snatched up by the feet, and taken flapping to the stump. Mom skillfully placed the chicken's head between the nails with one hand, and pulled the axe from its resting place with the other. Then, pulling on the chicken's feet to stretch the neck taut, Mom dealt a fatal blow that severed the head and sent the blood-spurting hen into frantic activity for a moment. Putting the axe back in the crevice, mom picked up the twitching hen and hung her upside down from the clothesline to bleed out. By dinner time, the hen's grisly remains had been transformed into a crispy, golden brown main course of fried chicken.

Taking care of one's personal business in those days meant

a trip to the outhouse. Ours had two holes to choose from, and a small window to let the daylight in. The sagging door had an inside latch for privacy. The latest Sears catalog served a dual purpose; entertainment to thumb through, then wipe with. During the hot, humid days of July and August, the outhouse became a suffocating gas chamber. If no one was nearby, the door stayed open, and the whole movement was accomplished quickly, without breathing if possible. Big brother Jay was always looking out for his little sisters; on the hottest days of summer, he would stop what he was doing when we called out, and stand guard, back turned to the open door, until we finished our business. In the cold of winter, we used bedroom chamber pots which were emptied in the outhouse the following morning. I preferred the stinky summer outhouse to the chamber pots. My route to the breakfast table took me past Dad's always-brimming pot, and its unspeakable contents.

There was no road from the nearby town of Paris Crossing to our farm. The only way in or out was on foot, along the railroad tracks. A deep hollow separated the farm from Paris Crossing. The hollow had been bridged with fill dirt years ago to carry the railroad tracks, which ran past our house ten feet or so above the level of the front door, and a mere fifty or so feet distant. The steam locomotives that shook the house several times a day were huge and frightening things. To keep us kids off the tracks and safe, the adults stoked our fears by telling us we would be sucked under the train and ground to bits if we failed to get far enough away when the locomotive passed.

The most impressive structure in Paris Crossing was the Dodd house. In the late 1930's it was converted into a funeral home. Everyone in Jennings County eventually ended up spending their last night above ground at the Dodd house. The house was a creepy, ivy covered, multi-story stone and brick mansion with a horse-drawn hearse in the garage, and for years, the only telephone in Paris Crossing. On those rare occasions when a call came in for someone in the family, one of the Dodd kids would run down the tracks to fetch us while the caller waited. The phone was located in a vestibule outside the viewing room, where a former neighbor occasionally lay in repose, surrounded by flowers and loud weeping.

Dodd Funeral Home

I went with Mom on her frequent trips into Paris Crossing, to Humphrey's Cash Store, where old men in coveralls sat on wooden crates out front, telling tales of the Great War, arguing about politics, and chewing Mail Pouch tobacco. "Loafers" mom would say disapprovingly; "Loafers with nothing better to do than sit around all day telling the same lies they told yesterday." Often present among the loafers was none other than Jesse Cook, my father. There was a story going around town that a well-dressed man from Indianapolis pulled up in front of the store one afternoon. Daddy was sitting on a produce crate with the others, twiddling his thumbs. The man from the city walked up to him and inquired snottily; "Do you just sit here doing this every day?" Dad spat out a wad of Mail Pouch, and replied; "No, sometimes I do this"…and reversed the direction of his twiddling. The man from the city shook his head in disgust, got back in his car, and sped off down Main Street. The old coots roared with laughter; fellow loafer Delbert Phyfer summed it up: "Jesse, you told that city feller to Go To Hell without so much as one cuss word!"

Humphrey's Cash Store 1929

Our farm, the woods, and Humphrey's Cash Store, provided all of life's needs. In town, we would purchase staples like flour and sugar, or maybe a special treat, like a candy bar, or a bottle of soda pop. Items not in stock in the store could be ordered there by catalog, and picked up a week or two later. Nearly all of the food that sustained us came from Daddy's garden, our cows and chickens, and the great dark woods that began near our farm, and went on forever. In the field between our house and the barn was Daddy's garden. The soil there was rich and black; the color and texture of chocolate cake. The rich soil produced wonderful crops of corn, carrots, string beans, and sweet, summer beefsteak tomatoes. We feasted on the bounty from Daddy's garden all summer long. What was left over was preserved in Mason jars and stored in the pantry for the cold months ahead. We ate well, and often. Dinner was the day's big meal, and was served in the middle of the day. We had a big breakfast in the morning, and a light meal of leftovers in the evening, which we called supper. There was no such thing as lunch.

Just beyond the farm house to the north was an open meadow, and beyond that, the woods; a dark, enchanted, forest of hardwood trees that seemed to go on forever. For those who knew where to look, the woods offered a treasure chest of delights; sassafras roots we used to make a delicious tea, walnut trees, blackberries from vines heaped thick on old fences, and strawberries from the dense patches that grew along the railroad tracks. A special mushroom appeared for a brief time in the spring. The whole family would take part in the treasure hunt, combing the woods for the long, spongey, Morels. Once back at the farmhouse, Mom would soak the sponges in warm water, and prepare a seasoned flour to coat them with. Frying produced a crunchy, golden brown crust that gave way to a gush of flavor when bitten into; delicious, and indescribable.

There was an enchanted place in the woods that we visited often. Here, a live spring flowed from a limestone cave creating a deep, quiet pond filled with life. We called it the Turtle Pond; named for the population of Snapping turtles that thrived there. If you approached the pond quietly and hid behind the trees, you would always catch a glimpse of several snappers hauled out on logs, or huge bullfrogs sunning themselves on the bank; and sometimes a colorful snake or two. Water snakes were abundant; they came in a variety of sizes and colors, and were a little creepy, but harmless. Far less common, but very dangerous, were the Water Moccasins and Copperheads. We kids were taught at an early age to identify and avoid them.

We learned how to fish at the Turtle Pond. Daddy fashioned cane poles, to which he would tie five or six feet of twine. A single hook was tied to the end of the line, and a colorful bobber fastened two feet above. Hooks were purchased from Humphrey's Cash Store. They came in a round tin like the containers that held snuff. Inside were hooks of various sizes. Bait was abundant; a shallow dig anywhere in Daddy's garden yielded handfuls of wriggling red worms. Grasshoppers and crickets also made great bait, and could be easily be caught in the pasture all summer long.

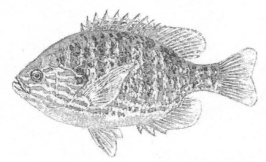

Turtle Pond Pumpkinseed

There were several kinds of fish in the Turtle Pond. The prettiest were the pumpkinseeds. They were not very big, but had bright, pumpkin-colored streaks on their bluish skin. The Green Sunfish were the most numerous, and were definitely the best bait thieves. The most sought-after eating fish were the Bluegill. They had sweet, white meat, and got bigger than the pumpkinseed or sunfish. We usually came home with a mess of Bluegill that would fill mom's cast iron skillet, and provide the whole family with a fried fish supper. The biggest fish in the pond were called Suckers, and they could grow to be several pounds in size. They had a reputation for being impossibly bony, so we threw them back on those rare occasions when they took the bait. It was a lot of fun catching the big Suckers. The cork bobber would twitch once or twice, sending off rings of ripples just before disappearing below the surface of the pond. It was a tug-o-war, and it took all of my strength to lift the silvery giants onto the bank, and stop their thrashing long enough for Daddy or Jay to remove the hook and release them.

Our family had very little money, and few possessions. To some folks, we were poor. I don't remember it that way; nearly every day of my early childhood was filled with moments of magic and wonder. Whole, natural, food was abundant year-round; no one ever went hungry. Our sturdy little farmhouse kept us warm in the winter and dry when summer afternoon downpours thundered on the metal roof. No one was ever lonely; the house was filled with the sounds of family. Our doors were never locked, there was nothing to fear. We had no television or radio. Without these distractions, I was freed to discover the little miracles happening all around me. I spent hours watching spiders weave complex webs, and bright-colored birds expertly construct their spring nests. It could be a hard life, but it was a good life, and I was happy.

2 JAY FREDERICK COOK

Relatives from Madison stopped by unexpectedly one sweltering morning in August, 1930. The couple had a son, Colin, the same age as Jay. The boys were cousins, and also great friends. I was a young child, so my memories of this time come in bits and pieces. As I recall, the family was returning from a summer reunion in Fort Wayne. They had over extended themselves, and were exhausted. They were invited to spend the night, and gladly accepted. It was a hot, humid summer. Violent afternoon thunder showers were a daily occurrence. At the same time every afternoon, black storm clouds would gather, blocking out the sun and turning everything dark. The wind would suddenly pick up from a dead calm, to be followed by a torrential downpour. It would all be over in an hour, leaving dreary sunshine and stifling humidity in its wake.

Jay shouldered most of the farm work that summer, as Daddy's health continued to deteriorate. He was a teen now, and eager to spend as much time as he could with his peers. Colin, the boy from Madison, was the same age as Jay. By the time the family had unloaded their luggage, the boys had already planned a campout at the Big Creek trestle; the local swimming hole. Big Creek flowed beneath the railroad tracks a mile or so south of Paris Crossing. Here, another stream we called Graham Creek joined to form the headwaters of the Muscatatuck River. A wooden trestle spanned the river gorge, providing a summer high dive for the local boys. The climb back up to the trestle, through a tunnel of poison ivy, was more dangerous than the dive. It was common to pay dearly for a refreshing afternoon swim with several days of intense itching. Big catfish were here for the boys who braved the dense thickets of poison ivy growing along the creek bank. There was a sandbar island that emerged during summer low water. The boys had a plan: They would camp overnight on the sandbar, catching catfish, telling ghost stories by the light of the kerosene lantern, and gorging on candy and soda pop packed in from Humphrey's Cash Store.

The boys sought and received permission from the grownups, on the condition that they return home by noon the following day. Jay sent Colin into the garden to dig up a coffee can full of worms. He then went to the barn, grabbed a lantern, cane fishing poles, and an old lunchbox full of hooks, weights, and bobbers. The next stop was Humphrey's Cash Store, where the boys pooled their pocket change: one dollar, and eighty cents. They left the store laden with their campout rations; cookies, soda pop, potato chips, and an assortment of candy bars. They reached the trestle in the early afternoon, made their way down the tunnel of poison ivy, and set up camp on the gravel bar in the middle of the creek. With camp made, the boys stripped to their underwear, climbed back up to the railroad tracks, and took an exhilarating plunge off the trestle into the cool water of Big Creek. That night, they sat around a campfire, crunching on potato chips and candy, and washing it all down with Big Red soda. It was the high point of summer for both boys. Colin came up with an idea; his family lived near Hanover Beach, and a popular swimming hole on the Ohio River that offered relief from the summer heat. It would be a full week before school started for the fall semester; Jay could come home with him for a final week of fun; it would be a well-deserved vacation away from the farm chores.

The boys returned the following morning, excited about the plan they had hatched around the sandbar campfire. They pled their case to the hesitant grownups. Eventually, Jay was given permission to go; he had worked like a trooper all summer long, and it was only fitting that he spend the last week of summer relaxing, and having fun. When the time came to leave, we all walked up the railroad tracks to see them off. Before climbing into the back seat of the car, Jay picked me up and gave me a hug. He reminded me that Matilda the goose was my responsibility until he returned, and extracted a promise from me that she would be fed and watered every day. The car pulled away, Jay waved through the back window. The car drove slowly down Main Street, and disappeared around the bend in front of the schoolhouse. That was the last time we would see Jay alive.

Jay drowned in the Ohio River the following day. We had no way of knowing Jay had died. There were no telephones in town yet. In the stifling late-afternoon heat, a lone figure appeared on the railroad tracks walking our way under blackening thunder clouds. He carried Jay's limp body in his arms. I remember cameos of Jay's dead body on the front room daybed where we had wrestled and giggled only two days earlier. Rain thundered on the metal roof; flashes of lightning lit the grim scene. Mom was lovingly washing Jay's face with water from a porcelain bowl; she dressed him in his Sunday best. He had an ugly furrow in his forearm where he had been bled. I was not quite four years old, which blessedly blunted the horror and grief of that moment somewhat. I would forever remember the scenes from this time clearly, but without emotion.

It would be nine more years before the Dodd family opened the first mortuary in Paris Crossing. Before Dodd's Funeral Home, the families of departed loved ones took care of burial preparations at home. Friends and relatives came to the house to pay their respects, and comfort the grieving family members. Jay lay on the daybed as if sleeping, arms crossed and hair combed, dressed in his Sunday suit, and covered to his waist with a quilt mom had made for his last birthday. All of Paris Crossing turned out that night. I remember lots of sniffles and weeping, and every so often, uproarious laughter as the townsfolk took turns recounting Jay's capers. Mrs. Hudson told the story of her poor milk cow: Dad sent Jay and his buddy to fetch a basket full of eggs from a farm on the far side of town. The route home took the boys past the Hudson's pasture, where a big brown and white Guernsey was grazing near the fence. Jay's buddy took an egg from the basket, threw it at the cow, and missed. Next, Jay took an egg from the basket on a dare; he scored a direct hit on the cow's backside. Within minutes, the basket was empty. Mrs. Hudson's Guernsey was a yolk-stained, dripping mess. The boys arrived back home with an empty basket, and an elaborate excuse that quickly came unraveled under cross-examination. There was a knock at the door; it was a very upset Mrs. Hudson. She had watched the whole thing unfold from her kitchen window. The boys were made to pay for the eggs, and go to the Hudson farm to bucket-wash the cow. Jay was given extra chores for the next week as punishment for his misleading story.

It was unusual for Jay to lie: Mom recalled the only other time he got in trouble for dishonesty. Jay lied to save a goose he had grown attached to. It was close to Christmas, and a special dinner was planned. Daddy ordered Jay to bring the goose to the killing stump. Jay had named the big goose Matilda after a popular song of the day. Instead of doing what he was told, Jay sneaked Matilda down to the spring below the barn. There, he fashioned a crude pen where the goose could hide out. Jay returned to the house claiming the goose was nowhere to be found; he offered a clump of white feathers as evidence that she was taken by a fox in the night. Two days later, Matilda escaped her hiding place by the spring, and came waddling up the path to the farmhouse right to where Daddy was standing. Jay was punished for lying, but succeeded in saving his pet goose.

Matilda

Jay was buried the following morning in the family plot at Coffee Creek. Sisters Florence and Genevieve had arrived late last evening. They were grief-stricken, but still managed to reach out to comfort me and Alice. It was more than the loss of our beloved big brother that shook us deeply; we were still children, and were bewildered and frightened by this new reality, that life ends with death. Jay's gravesite overlooked the slow-moving Coffee Creek, and the green, rolling farmland of Jennings County beyond. The gathering of friends and relatives listened with heads bowed as the Pastor delivered a comforting message of Christ's promise of eternal life. While the Pastor's prayer droned on, I opened my eyes to look around. My attention was drawn to a cottontail rabbit sitting amid the gravestones not far away, staring in my direction. How strange, I thought. We made eye contact. The bunny rose up onto its hind feet, and paddled its paws furiously for just a moment. I thought I saw the rabbit smile; it twitched its whiskers in a comical way, and then hopped behind a headstone and disappeared. Jay, I thought; that show was for me and me alone. I felt a rush of joy in that moment. I instantly somehow knew that some part of Jay never died, and all was well.

Among all of my memories of that day, I find none of Daddy.
I don't have a single image of him at the Coffee Creek
cemetery that day. Sister Florence told me later in life that
Daddy was never the same after Jay's death. Daddy had
survived a hardscrabble youth after losing his father at an
early age. His widowed mother was impoverished, and had
to ask a sister to take her in along with her two sons, Charlie
and Jesse. Starting life with nothing to his name, Daddy
managed to build a good life in Paris Crossing, raise good
children who adored him, and be surrounded by friends who
enjoyed his company. He was blessed with a son who was
his shining pride and joy; a son to carry on the Cook name.
Daddy was not a spiritual man; he had no cushion to absorb
the blow of Jay's death; he was crushed, and his spirit
broken.

3 THANKSGIVING MEMORIES 1935

Autumn in Indiana is a beautiful time of year. The woods are suddenly ablaze with color. Yellow, gold and red leaves adorn the trees, and fall into deep piles on the ground below. The sun shines lower in the sky, and the air becomes still. The muggy heat of summer is a distant memory now, and we teeter on the brink of winter for a few magic days. The nights become clear and cold. Quilts and thick blankets come out of the closets. The wood stove glows to life again. With cool weather comes the hunting season, the harvesting of game from the surrounding woods, and the butchering of hogs and cattle. Butchering an animal was a community affair. Daddy would often leave on October mornings to assist neighbors in the slaughtering process. He always returned at the end of the day with several pounds of beef or pork for the icebox; his reward for being a good neighbor.

It had been five years since we lost Jay. Daddy's health continued to decline, requiring Alice and I shoulder more of the routine farm chores. We collected eggs, fetched water, and took trash to the burn pit. At the age of eight, I learned to help with the fall rabbit hunt. On the day after the first frost, we set our traps along the stream at the bottom of the hollow that lay between the farmhouse and town. Daddy would stop at signs of recent rabbit activity, and pull a snare from his pocket. The snare was a piece of wire formed into a loop, and attached to a few feet of sturdy cord. The loop would be opened into a circle big enough for the rabbit to slip its head into, and then hidden beneath twigs and leaves. In the middle of the loop, we placed a piece of carrot for bait. Daddy would then secure the end of the cord to a wooden stake he had pounded into the ground with his hand axe. After we had positioned all of our snares, we headed back up the hill to the house for supper and bedtime.

At the break of day, I would don my warmest clothes, pull on my mittens, and set off to check the traps. It was always colder at the bottom of the hollow. The little stream that flows through the bottom was usually frozen solid enough for me to stand on. I remember seeing my breath in the cold morning air, puffing through streamside thickets, trying to recall where we had set our traps. I carried a pocketful of carrot pieces in my coat to rebait empty snares. Clever rabbits knew how to get the bait without suffering the consequences. Some mornings there were lots of clever rabbits, and no food for our table. Usually though, I came upon at least one fat cottontail that had fallen for our trickery. I would squeal with delight, but always followed my celebration with a quiet prayer of thanks for the rabbit that would now nourish our family.

It made me feel good to see Daddy's smile of approval when I returned from a successful hunt. He worked hard to provide our family with life's needs. That fact more than made up for his quick temper, and frequent use of cuss words. Daddy's vocabulary of cuss words was extensive. He was a brilliant arranger of creative profanity, which he bellowed with undeniable sincerity when provoked.

I remember the day I was sent to town to buy door hinges for a new chicken coop. Daddy was pounding nails in the new coop when the hammer missed the nail, and came down on his thumb instead. A faint blast of loud profanity made it across the hollow and rolled down the main street of town, reaching my ears about the same time as the old men loafing in front of Humphrey's Cash Store. I blushed as crusty laughter erupted from the old coots in coveralls. Delbert Phyfer spat out a mouthful of Mail Pouch chewing tobacco, and spoke for the group; "Well sir, that's Jesse Cook, I reckon!" The other loafers grinned, spat, and bobbed their heads in agreement.

Grandma Emma Humphrey and the Humphrey House

The high point of autumn was the Humphrey family Thanksgiving, held at my Grandma's house on Main Street. My two older sisters had long ago married, and moved to the city. This was one of the special holidays I got to be with them again. Sister Genevieve had settled in the town of Columbus. She always brought me nice things to wear, and her husband Hube treated me like his own little sister. He always took time to play with me and make me laugh with his corny jokes. Sister Florence bought a house in far-away Indianapolis. She was the eldest sibling. Florence could be bossy, but that never bothered me. I looked up to her, and knew her commands and corrections came from a deep love and concern for my well-being. Florence was married to Ernie Schill, a handsome man from nearby Crothersville. Uncle Ernie had been working for the railroad since lying about his age to get hired at 15. Ernie chain-smoked cigarettes, and played the guitar. He loved Buicks. Every other year, in September, he and Florence would take a weeklong road trip to Detroit to trade in their old Buick for a new one. The family always got to ride in the new car at Thanksgiving. By then, it would reek of cigarette smoke just like the Buicks before it. Alice was a teenager now. We shared a room and fought constantly. Alice was very pretty, and all the boys were chasing after her. It didn't matter to the love-struck boys that she was usually very grumpy, fought with Daddy all the time, and had a mean streak that I alone was privileged to see.

My mother, Anna Humphrey Cook, was the granddaughter of a merchant from Brighton, England who came to the United States in 1864. WG Humphrey settled in Paris Crossing, where he built the town's first General Store in 1869. The family prospered and multiplied there. Five generations of Humphreys maintained the store. Shortly after the store was sold to a new owner, it was destroyed by a fire of suspicious origin.

Mom was very English; she was stoic, and maintained a "stiff upper lip" during good times and bad. She endured the many hardships of rural life without complaint. She dealt with tragedy, including the loss of her only son, with the same quiet, inner strength. I believe the source of her resolute nature was her mother, whose life story was fascinating, and tragic.

My maternal grandmother was born Emily Smith in 1865. She was conceived the night before her father, William B. Smith, left to join Union forces protecting the railroad trestle at Sulphur Springs, Alabama, from rebel saboteurs. In an ensuing battle, the Union position was overrun. William was captured, and sent to the Confederate prison camp near Andersonville, Georgia. When the war ended in 1865, the prisoners who had survived rampant disease and starvation in the camp were marched to Vicksburg, Mississippi.

William boarded the Sultana, a side-wheeler conscripted by the Union to take the soldiers up-river. The Sultana was built to accommodate 400 passengers and crew. When the boat left Vicksburg, there were 2,400 aboard. Two days later, just above Memphis, the Sultana exploded in the night, and burned to the waterline. Over 1,500 lives were lost. Grandma's dad, my great grandfather William B. Smith, was never found. The greatest maritime disaster in our country's history was pushed off the front page by a bigger news story: The assassination of President Lincoln one week earlier.

Daddy had an older brother, Charles. He lived in a river town, a short distance to the south. He and Daddy were very different people. Uncle Charlie was soft-spoken and kind; he was a store keeper by profession. He lived and worked in the beautiful Ohio River town of Madison. Charlie was married to a mean-spirited, controlling nag, who together with her resident spinster sister, did all they could to make poor Charlie's life a miserable, hen-pecked ordeal. It was a great pleasure of mine to cheer him up with little gifts I had fashioned with my own hands. I took to doing this whenever we would see each other. His appreciation was sincere, and my great reward was hearing him say "I love you little girl" when our time to visit was done. I longed to see him this Thanksgiving, but would not, as our celebration this day would be with the Humphrey clan, Mom's side of the family.

Willa Jane was the same age as me, and my favorite cousin. Her father was Delbert Phyfer, Daddy's brother in law, and fellow Main Street loafer. Willa Jane's mother, my aunt, had tragically died young. Grandma Humphrey didn't approve of Delbert's ways.   She didn't want her granddaughter to be influenced by her son in law, who she considered a lazy, Mail Pouch-chewing deadbeat. After her mom died, Willa Jane came to live with Grandma Humphrey. Delbert, distraught over the loss of his young wife, agreed it would be best.

On this Thanksgiving Day, Willa Jane and I ventured into the attic as always. It was our fantasyland up there.   A big steamer trunk at the far end of the attic was our fort. Inside the trunk was Grandma's musty wedding gown. We clowned around in the gown. We played damsels in distress, climbing in and out of our trunk fortress. A call came from downstairs for Willa Jane; she hopped out of the trunk, and closed the lid. I rose up to follow but the lid wouldn't budge; I was locked in. I waited patiently for my cousin to return. After a few minutes of waiting in the dark, panic began to set in. I was trapped; what if Willa Jane forgot about me and never came back? I would slowly suffocate in the air tight trunk, alone and in the dark. I pushed against the trunk lid with all my might; I cried out hoping someone downstairs would hear me. I was panicky, and on the verge of tears when the image of the cemetery bunny came to mind.

A rush of deep peace accompanied the image; I plopped down on my back, and stretched out, staring into the darkness. A flood of comforting thoughts drew me inside; I was whisked away to a bright place of love and warmth. For the rest of my life, in my darkest hours when I was at the end of my rope, I would experience this peace that came as a force beyond thought. After becoming a Christian much later in life, I identified this comforting force as the Holy Spirit Christ spoke of.

I was drawn out of my reverie by the sound of muffled voices. The trunk lid flew open; I blinked and squinted in the sudden daylight. I heard sighs of relief from the adults who had come with Willa Jane to free me. She had been called down to help set the table for dinner, not aware that she had locked me the trunk. Willa Jane finished setting the table, and went to join our cousins playing on the front lawn; she had forgotten all about me. The family was half way through Thanksgiving dinner when Uncle Hube asked "Where's Betty Lou?" A moment later a rescue party rumbled up the narrow stairs with Willa Jane in the lead. All were relieved to find me safe and sound, and surprised to find me calmly staring up at them from the floor of the trunk, smiling, peaceful, relaxed, and very hungry. We all rumbled back down the stairs to the dining room. Uncle Hube gave me his seat at the head of the table, and personally served me.

I was old news real quick. I was safe and accounted for. Everyone went on with the conversations my crisis had interrupted. I now became a little invisible fly on the wall, chomping away on my food at the head of the table, watching the others...listening in to my choice of several intense conversations that had resumed around the table: All the men in the family were huge baseball fans. In southeast Indiana, the big league team most folks pulled for was the Cincinnati Reds. Up until this season, all big league games were played during daylight hours. The 1935 season had seen the first night time game ever played, at Crosley Field in Cincinnati. My uncles were sharply divided over whether playing night ball was proper. The great Babe Ruth retired after the 1935 season, sending Uncle Fritz into a rant about his beloved New York Yankees not allowing the Babe to finish his career in a Yankee uniform. I remember hearing the name Adolph Hitler for the first time when the conversation turned from baseball to politics.

The memorable Thanksgiving wrapped up with a group prayer for young Rupert Law, a local boy who had suffered a terrible injury last summer. Rupert was fourteen years old. He was helping his father dig a new well on the Law farm, a nice spread midway between Paris Crossing and Commiskey. Some loose earth gave way at the top of the well, dropping a melon-size rock on top of his head, and burying him under a foot of mud and debris. Rupert was home from the hospital now, but he was not the same person as before. Only time would tell if he would regain his coordination and reasoning ability. We said a special prayer for Rupert's father, who was beside himself with guilt; he blamed himself for the tragedy that had altered the course of his only son's life, perhaps forever. The Humphrey Thanksgiving always concluded with a prayer circle wherein we all shared one thing we were thankful for, and then prayed together that all would be kept in God's protective grace, and be back in a year for another family Thanksgiving.

4 THE BEER TRAIN

Baltimore & Ohio 4-8-2 Steam Locomotive,

The Cook farmhouse was built in 1870 by my mother's family, the Humphreys. Years later, the railroad came to town. The Cook farmhouse was nearly in the middle of the new railway's best approach to Paris Crossing. Relocating the house was not an option, resulting in the new tracks being put down ridiculously close to the front of the house where my bedroom was located. It was a busy route; several passenger trains rumbled by every day, followed by the freight trains at night. There was a nightly freight train from North Vernon to Louisville. I will never forget it. The beast rumbled through Paris Crossing every day at midnight. The locomotives that pulled the trains in that day were black, smoke-puffing monsters with one bright headlight that would cast a spotlight across my bedroom wall every night as the train approached. For that one terrifying moment, the behemoth was coming directly at our house, directly at my bedroom where I cowered beneath the covers.   A shrill whistle blast would come next. Gradually, the bedroom would fall dark again as the tracks curved away to pass by our house. A frightening rumble shook my bed as the monster approached. Then, the locomotive would fly by in a thunderous whoosh, making my bed tremble, and the tracks go clickity-clackity-clickity-clack as they flexed and bent under the weight of the box cars.

The passenger trains normally came by during daylight hours. Four a day came by the house when I was younger; two southbound and two headed north. I have fond memories of a kind porter who rode in the caboose of one of the passenger trains. The first train south every Monday made a brief stop in Paris Crossing. The caboose would be parked just above our house for five minutes or so while mail and passengers were loaded into the front of the train in town. I would often go outside with Mom to wave at the porter who always came out of the caboose to stand on the little railed-in porch. We were close enough for Mom and the Porter to say hello and chat a bit before the train lurched forward to resume the trip to Louisville. It got to be a regular thing; every Monday the southbound passenger train stopped in Paris Crossing, and we would be waiting for it.

One Monday morning I was feeling poorly with a nasty cold, and missed seeing our friend on the caboose. Later in the morning I was feeling better, and went to play in the front yard. Something caught my eye on the grassy bank; it was a Hershey bar. It was the king size chocolate bar; it looked huge in my little hands. From that day forward, every Monday, the porter would come out on his porch and wave, then sail a king size Hershey bar down to where I stood on the lawn by the front door. It was a great disappointment when, not long after, the trains no longer stopped in Paris

Crossing. The mail pickup was automated; the speeding train now snatched the mailbag from a pole alongside the tracks. I never knew the porter's name, but I never forgot his simple act of kind thoughtfulness.

I eventually got used to the trains being a part of my daily life. My fear subsided over the years as train after train passed by the house without incident. Then, one night when I was in high school, the unthinkable finally happened: minutes after passing our house in Paris Crossing, the midnight locomotive flew off the tracks at the Big Creek trestle, and plunged down into the ravine, taking its long string of loaded boxcars and tankers with it. The tons of steel thudding deep into the riverbank mud shook the earth, and a low rumble that seemed to go on forever woke up everyone in Jennings and Jefferson County.

The first people on the scene that night were amazed to find that no one had died. Clyde Gray, the engineer, had been burned by acid leaking from one of the twisted tanker cars, but he was alive. Folks first on the scene found a dazed Clyde walking around the wreckage, inspecting the damage by lantern light. Clyde, a life-long resident of nearby North Vernon, was taken to a hospital in Indianapolis for treatment of chemical burns. There, to everyone's sad surprise, he died a few days later.

Events out of the ordinary rarely happened in our little corner of the world. Word of the train wreck spread quickly; everyone wanted to see it firsthand. At the break of dawn, local townsfolk were making the trek down the railroad tracks to view the carnage below the Big Creek trestle. There, at the confluence of Graham Creek and Big Creek, a mountain of twisted railroad cars had created a dam across Big Creek, causing a large lake to form behind the wreck where

Graham Creek used to be. Big Creek below the dam was reduced to a small stream of yellowish fluid leaking from several punctured tanker cars. Standing on end, half buried in the riverbank mud, the locomotive stood above the wreckage, its coal car still coupled, dangling in the air with its contents strewn about on the creek bank below.

Three of the boxcars lying on the creek bed were emblazoned with the distinctive Blatz beer logo. Early gawkers returning from the trestle brought back the news that several hundred cases of Blatz beer had survived the crash, and were now free for the taking. The news of free beer spread like wildfire, and mobilized the boys of Jefferson, and Jennings Counties. The rowdy Malcom boys from Lovett pulled together a team, and drew up a plan. They would drive the backroads to Paris Crossing with four wheelbarrows stacked on the bed of their father's farm truck. From there, they planned to go in on foot, get into the boxcars, and bucket-brigade the cases of beer up to the waiting wheelbarrows. They would return along the tracks to the truck parked back in Paris Crossing, load the beer and wheelbarrows onto the flatbed, and be home before dawn.

Meanwhile, a similar plan was being hatched by some Deputy boys; they also cooked up a nocturnal mission, using a handcar they would appropriate from a Deputy Station siding. Except for the means of transport, their plan was basically the same as the Lovett team; pump the handcar to the trestle, find the beer, bucket-brigade the cases out of the ravine, and return to the Deputy Station with the booty. Once there, offload the beer into a waiting wagon, and return the handcar to its siding. Time was of the essence. It had been several hours since the train flew off the rails; very soon, accident investigators would be crawling all over the wreckage. The decision was made to go that night. Up in Lovett, the Malcom boys had reached the same conclusion; they too were going in.

For the Malcom boys coming south from Lovett, and the Deputy boys on their handcar coming north, everything went smoothly, and according to plan. They converged on the trestle from opposite directions around midnight. After a short-lived standoff of pushing and shoving, the teams agreed to share the wealth; after all, there was more than enough beer to go around. They made their way by flashlight through the tunnel of poison ivy leading down to the creek bed. Their lanterns and flashlights illuminated the ghastly wall of twisted steel at the bottom of the ravine. Two of the Blatz boxcars were lying on their side with tons of wreckage piled on top; the vast wealth of beer they held inside, totally inaccessible. A little further downstream the third Blatz boxcar stood upright, its wheels sunk deep into the mud. The boys whooped with delight at the sight of easy pickings. They rounded the boxcar with flashlights and lanterns, looking for the sliding access door. One of the Lovett boys was the first to illuminate the boxcar door with his flashlight; it was wide open. The edge of the door was splintered. Closer examination revealed an explosive charge had been detonated to blow off the door lock. The boxcar was empty, except for several dozen loose cans of Blatz scattered here and there on the floor. The boys uttered a few profanities, shrugged, and began dividing up what was left of the beer. Back up on the trestle, the Lovett and Deputy boys, now friends and partners in crime, paused for a beer together before heading off in opposite directions. The oldest Malcom boy proposed a toast, and new joint venture: To finding whoever beat them to the beer, and thoroughly kicking their asses.

The Notorious Phillips Boys

The notorious Phillips brothers lived on a farm south of Deputy. They were very familiar with the local creeks. One of their favorite fishing holes was below the Big Creek trestle; the site of the train wreck. The brothers had a flat-bottom Jon boat they kept under the Highway 3 Bridge over Big Creek. From here, it was a short trip downstream to the railroad trestle.

The Phillips boys' bait of choice was dynamite, which they pilfered from their father's shed. Explosives were commonly used in farming communities to clear tree stumps or boulders when preparing land for the planting of crops. The Phillips boys soon discovered dynamite to be vastly more efficient than worms in filling a boat with fish. Here's how it worked: They only fished at night. The boys left the Highway 3 Bridge in the Jon boat at sunset, and rowed downstream to the trestle. Upon arrival at the fishing hole, big brother Myron would take up his position in the middle of the trestle. When his brothers reached a safe distance downstream, he lit the dynamite and dropped it into the middle of Big Creek. A muffled explosion followed, creating a waterspout that sprayed Myron on the trestle above. Downstream, in the circle of light created by kerosene lanterns, the brothers waded in to retrieve the largest of the hundreds of stunned fish that floated by in the slow-moving current. In a couple of hours the boys were back at the Highway 3 Bridge with a Jon boat full of catfish, bass, and drum.

The Phillips family had been shaken awake by a mysterious, distant rumble in the night. News that it was a train wreck reached the farm early in the morning. Myron was sent into town on an errand later that afternoon. He was filling a bag with nails from a bin at Deputy Hardware, when he heard a lively whispered conversation coming from the next aisle over; it was two of the Deputy boys buying supplies for the beer caper. They inadvertently told Myron everything he needed to know; he raced home to share his findings with his younger brothers.

By sunset that evening, the boys were boarding their Jon boat for the trip downriver to the trestle. They carried lanterns, wading boots, and a small charge of dynamite. At the wreck site, they discovered that only one of the three Blatz boxcars was accessible. Myron skillfully set a charge that blew off the leading edge of the wooden door, taking the steel hasp with it. Carrying three cases at a time, the boys loaded the beer into the Jon boat parked just upstream from the wreckage. When the boat was close to sinking under the load, the boys pulled on their wading boots. They took up positions along the gunwales to steady the boat, and started the slow walk through the shallows back to the Highway 3 Bridge.

It would be a gross understatement to say that father Gene Phillips would not approve of stealing a Jon boat full of beer; once home, the booty would have to be hidden. Working quietly in the dark, the boys split up their haul, and stashed the Blatz in several locations around the farm. There was a shallow ditch along the edge of the plowed field nearest the house. The boys lined up several cases of Blatz the length of the ditch, and covered them with a shallow layer of dirt. The remaining cases of beer were stashed in the hayloft behind large burlap bags of chicken scratch. Ironically, the Phillips brothers didn't drink beer; it was the excitement of the caper that was the primary allure for Charles and Kenny. Enterprising Myron, on the other hand, saw the beer as an opportunity to make some money. He was saving for a car; a Ford coupe that the girls would line up to ride in. The last case of beer went into hiding at the stroke of midnight; the deed was done. Meanwhile, back at the trestle, the losing beer recovery teams from Deputy and Lovett were about to discover they'd been had.

5 THE HIGH SCHOOL YEARS

Paris Crossing Girls; Betty Lou (2nd from Left) and Alice (far Right)

Coming of age in rural Indiana presented new challenges: There were very few places for boys and girls to gather and meet outside the home. There was no place to take a date; no movie theatres, or restaurants. Our social lives revolved around school and church activities. The church offered regular summer picnics and softball games. In the colder months, there were holiday programs, and weekly potluck dinners. We had softball and basketball teams, and played other churches from surrounding communities. The men from the Coffee Creek congregation had bladed off a baseball diamond in a large clearing near the cemetery. A backstop made of chicken wire and fence posts protected fans from foul balls and errant throws. The ladies ran a concession stand from a flatbed truck serving hot dogs, popcorn, and Big Red. These were great events for meeting new boys, or making new girlfriends.

We had a beautiful schoolhouse. It was a two-story brick building that sat in a large clearing at the end of Main Street, surrounded by a hardwood forest. Two classrooms on the ground floor were dedicated to the elementary grades; the upstairs was all high school. We were the Paris Crossing Pirates, with a menacing yellow and black mascot who wore an eyepatch and clenched a dagger between his stained teeth. Our graduating class of 1945 numbered 21; ten boys, and eleven girls.

We had three or four school dances every year, and made frequent field trips to local points of interest. Our basketball team was very good. Basketball in Indiana was a really big deal; far and away the most popular sport statewide. Every person in town turned out for local high school games. We battled with the neighboring villages for bragging rights. They were noisy and rowdy affairs, and a great place to meet new friends, or make new enemies.

We heard of plans to build a roller skating rink in Paris Crossing.   The news created great excitement among the young folks. I was in my first year of high school when the long-awaited skating rink opened its doors for the first time. On that first night, there was standing room only; the new rink was packed to the rafters. Young and old alike, from the nearby towns of Deputy, Crothersville, Lovett, and Commiskey, came to be a part of the excitement.

Paris Crossing Schoolhouse

My whole family went to town together for the Grand
Opening. I crammed into the crowded bleachers with Mom,
Dad, and Alice. The gleaming hardwood floor was flanked by
wooden bleachers. At the far end of the building, a man in a
wooden booth was setting up a record player; two big
speakers hung from the wall above the booth. At the
opposite end of the rink, a low wall separated the hardwood
floor from a carpeted area where skates could be rented and
laced on. Near the skate rental counter there was an open
Dutch door which led into to a small kitchen. The sound and
aroma of popping corn wafted through the open door. A
brown bag full of hot popcorn and a bottle of Big Red could
be had there for a nickel.

A special performance by a pair of professional skaters from
Indianapolis highlighted the Grand Opening gala. As soon
as the last straggler found a seat in the packed bleachers,
the house lights began to dim. Festive music boomed forth
from the speakers at the end of the rink. A spotlight from the
ceiling illuminated two figures waiting in the dark at the far
end of the rink. The music went silent; the young couple

glided onto the hardwood floor, and stopped in the center of the rink to acknowledge the applause. A scratchy selection from the Nutcracker Suite began playing softly. The couple turned to face each other, then joined hands and glided effortlessly, gracefully, around the hardwood oval. They skated forward, then backwards, then forward again; it was poetry in motion to me.

I was instantly hooked on roller skating, and I hadn't even put on a pair of skates yet. The couple completed their program, returned to the center of the floor, and stopped. They waved to the cheering crowd, and skated back to the far end of the rink. There would be no public skating this night. We were all invited to come onto the hardwood floor and meet the brilliant professionals who had just wowed us with their seamless routine.

A long line formed in front of the Dutch door for popcorn and soda pop. I went to the carpeted area to examine a pair of skates from the rental rack. All the skates were brand new, and beautiful. I had some money saved up from a summer job at a Madison packing plant. I didn't have enough for a new pair of skates, but I had a good start.

The Paris Crossing skating rink quickly became the place to be, and be seen. One month after the grand opening, the hardwood floor was packed with skaters every Saturday night. I learned my basic moves on rented skates. I took to it right away; in a matter of weeks, I was flying gracefully around the hardwood oval. I quickly became quite good at skating solo. I was ready to move on to couples skating. I began paying attention to the older couples who came to the rink with years of experience skating elsewhere. I found it very romantic; like dancing, only better. Time on the floor was divided between solo skating, and couples. The rink master called out the change every hour or so. The boys were allowed a minute or two to secure a partner, then the music started up again. On Sadie Hawkins nights, the girls got to go after the boys.

I practiced the moves I learned from closely watching the older couples. When I finally felt comfortable enough, I started making myself available for the couples skate instead of running to the snack bar for a Big Red. So there I sat, nervously waiting for the first boy to come over and ask me to skate. There was an older boy, one of several who always came looking for my big sister, Alice. He was the oldest of the notorious Phillips boys. On this occasion, he wasn't quick enough getting to Alice and lost out to another suitor. He turned to me and extended his hand. He was a little guy, but very handsome, and he could skate like the wind. His name was Myron. He had his own car; a shiny red and black 1936 Ford, and he fancied himself as quite the Lady's Man. He was too old for me, but I found him funny and charming, and looked forward to skating with him every Saturday. Before long, he no longer sought Alice; he came straight for me instead of my beautiful big sister.

Myron had just bought his flashy Ford; it was the first car ever owned by the Phillips family. The car was his pride and joy. He would not allow his brothers to ride in the car, lest they stain the upholstery, or foul the floor mats with their muddy shoes. On skate nights, brothers Kenneth and Charles were forced to walk along the railroad tracks to the Paris Crossing rink from their farm in Deputy. They would arrive late, with wind-mussed hair, and briers in their socks. At the end of the evening when the rink closed, Myron motored down Main Street to Highway 3 for the short drive to

Deputy. At the same time, his younger brothers set off on foot along the dark railroad tracks for the long walk home.

Charles was slight in stature like his brother Myron, and just as handsome: Kenny was the husky one, and to me, the best looking of them all; wavy red hair, and soft blue eyes, a fact that did not go unnoticed by the girls of Paris Crossing. I found myself nervously glancing at the front door of the rink every Saturday night waiting for Kenny to appear with his brother Charles. I got instant tummy butterflies when they finally came through the door. You wouldn't have known to look at me; I worked very hard to act disinterested and aloof, when in fact I was anything but.

I inquired behind the scenes about the notorious Phillips boys: I knew a few girls who attended Deputy High School, or worshipped at the Deputy Methodist church; they all knew the family well. I learned that the Phillips family lived on a farm south of Deputy, about five miles from Paris Crossing. The boys had three sisters. Their mother's name was Cammie. My friends all said the same thing; Cammie was an expressive and loving woman who was imbued with the Gift of Gab. Father Eugene was a teacher, farmer, and former prohibitionist. Eugene maintained several milk cows, a hog pen, a flock of laying hens, and 2 draft horses. He grew corn, tomatoes, potatoes, and an assortment of other vegetables in the summer. In the winter months, he wrote Sunday school lesson plans, and taught English at Deputy High School.

The following Saturday I took my usual place in the bleachers facing the door, and waited for Kenny and his brother Charles to appear. Myron had not arrived yet. That was very unusual; he was always the first Phillips brother to arrive, well ahead of the others. To my great surprise all three brothers came through the door together a few minutes later. There stood the impeccable Myron, looking like an unmade bed, with wind-mussed hair and briers festooned on his socks and pant legs. Kenny left his brothers standing at the door, and came straight to the bleachers where I was now laughing aloud. He plopped down beside me, and quietly began picking the foxtails from his socks and trousers. My tummy butterflies were swarming. We talked beyond a nervous "hello" for the first time that night. Kenny never left my side. We never even put our skates on. Initial awkward moments quickly gave way to giddy giggles and blushing. We were oblivious to the knowing grins of our friends as they rolled past the bleachers were we sat. While the music played and the others skated by, Kenny explained to me what had happened:

A few days back, while dragging a disc plow at the edge of his field, his father Gene hit something sharp that damaged one of the tractor's two front tires. As he dismounted to take a closer look, a metallic glint in the plowed dirt behind the tractor caught his eye. He got down on his knees and unearthed the metal object; it was a crumpled can of Blatz beer. He dug further and found another Blatz can, then another, and then another.

Gene had to go into Deputy to get a new tractor tire. He couldn't wait to tell his remarkable story. Outside Deputy Hardware, Gene pulled up a crate and joined the half-dozen loafers in coveralls. He told his story: It was a miracle, he joked; he had somehow managed to grow beer without planting a single seed! The old men spat out their chew, and erupted in laughter. By early afternoon Gene was back at the farm with a new tractor tire. He needed a jack; his son Myron's new Ford sat at the end of the gravel driveway.

Gene popped the trunk lid to retrieve the car's bumper jack. Inside the trunk, he found another cache of Blatz beer. Myron had just loaded the beer from his stash in the barn hayloft for delivery to the Lovett General Store where he had struck a deal the day before. The jig was up; father Gene called out for his son. Myron had been hiding behind the kitchen screen door watching everything unfold, and desperately trying to fabricate a plausible explanation. He came up empty-handed.

Myron emerged from the house with nervous sweat beading up on his forehead, and an inappropriate, guilty, ear-to-ear grin. On foot, the most direct route to the skating rink was along the railroad tracks. Kenny and Charles knew this well. Myron would now discover this too. His shiny red and black Ford was covered with a canvas drop cloth, and parked in a corner of the barn...indefinitely.

It was Myron who broke the trance and brought us back to earth when he came to fetch his brother at closing time. He approached us with a sly grin, skates slung over his shoulder. It was time to begin the long walk home. I parted company with Kenny and his brothers at the Main Street railroad crossing. I headed back home along the tracks in the opposite direction, floating on air. Mom greeted me at the front door, eager to hear about my evening. We took a seat next to each other on the front room daybed. We spoke softly so as not to wake Daddy.

I proceeded to gush out the details of the best day of my life so far. Mom listened patiently then gave me the "birds and bees" lecture she had perfected on my three older sisters. Learning I was getting involved with a Phillips boy was doubtless a cause for mild concern. The Phillips family was well known in the local townships. Father Gene was widely respected. Many of the townsfolk had been a student in his Sunday school class, or knew him from his teaching at Deputy High School. His three daughters were sweet, and well-mannered. His sons were good boys, but infamous for their rascally capers; fishing with dynamite, cow tipping, things like that.

I was soon seeing Kenny every weekend. I invited him to come to church with our family, which went over well with both sets of parents. The Coffee Creek Baptist Church in Paris Crossing was the Cook and Humphrey families' church home. For nearly a century it had been their house of worship, and the site of many family weddings and funerals. It became my Sunday routine to meet Kenny on the railroad tracks, and walk hand-in-hand to the church for morning service. Potluck socials followed worship every Sunday. We were now spending every weekend together. Kenny would come early on Saturdays so we had time together before his brothers arrived for skating. I usually walked to the Big Creek trestle to meet him.

When Myron eventually got his Ford back, it was on the condition that his brothers would ride too. A contrite Myron humbly agreed, and was soon bringing Kenny over to Paris Crossing anytime we needed to see each other, which was nearly every day. He knew, as I did, that his brother would soon be leaving us to go to war. World War II was in full swing, and it was expected that the boys in the 1945 graduating class would be drafted into military service very soon after receiving their diplomas. As graduation day grew near, I dreaded the day when we would have to say goodbye; perhaps forever. It was a tremendous relief when the war ended in the late summer after our graduation. The military still had much to do even though the fighting was over. The draft continued on, and eventually Kenny had to go. By that time, it was common knowledge in the neighborhood that Kenny and I had become a couple. We were starting to talk about a future together; marriage, family, and moving to a home of our own in the city like my sisters before us. The farm life we and generations before us had lived was coming to an end. Cities were the way of the future; it was a worrisome but exciting time to be alive.

BETTY LOU COOK 1945

6 THE ARMY YEARS

Kenny was drafted into the Army at the end of 1945. The war in Europe had ended in May of that year. The Japanese surrendered the following September, marking the end of World War II. Kenny reported to Fort Benjamin Harrison in December to begin basic training. Following a two-week furlough in March, 1946, he was sent to Europe to join the US occupation forces, where he was assigned to a permanent duty station in Antwerp, Belgium.

Private Kenny with Parents and Nieces

The day Kenny left for basic training was filled with tears and sadness. He was only going about eighty miles away from home, to an army base near Indianapolis. What I was really dreading was the two-year deployment that would follow. After three long months, Kenny stepped off the Greyhound bus in North Vernon, looking handsome and fit in his Army uniform. I was all a-twitter after three months of nothing but an occasional letter. A romantic whirlwind ensued, culminating with our presence before the Justice of Peace at the North Vernon courthouse. There, we were married in a small ceremony attended only by close family members. We enjoyed a short honeymoon, and then he was gone.

I was out of High School now, and ready to join the workforce in whatever capacity I could. Job opportunities were very limited in the small towns around Paris Crossing. Sister Florence convinced me to come live with her in the city. The post-war economy was booming, and jobs were plentiful. Three months after Kenny returned to Europe, I moved into Florence and Ernie's house on North Colorado Street in Indianapolis. I had the upstairs loft all to myself. The house reeked of Ernie's cigarette smoke, but it didn't bother me. The truth was, my sisters and I were a rarity in that we were all non- smokers. Most of the people we knew smoked cigarettes in those days. Smokers were free to lite up anywhere; theatres, restaurants, buses, hospitals; any public place. I had grown used to it, but Ernie's four packs a day habit took it to a new level.

It only took a week to land a job as an assembler trainee at Arvin, a company that made household appliances. I learned to assemble toasters and steam irons, and learned soldering techniques that I would use in the future to make circuit boards. I developed friendships with other young women whose men were also overseas mopping up after the war. It was very exciting being in a big city for the first time. There were movie theatres, restaurants, and clubs, and they all stayed open after the sun went down. I had new friends at work, a loving home with my sister and brother-in-law, and a good income from a job I enjoyed: Life was good!

I had gotten to know the Army wife who shared my workspace. She was my age, and also had a husband overseas. She suggested we get together for a movie after work. *The Postman Always Rings Twice* was a popular film that year; it was showing at a theatre near the Arvin plant. This was pretty exciting for me. I had never watched a movie in a theatre before. On Friday, we rode the bus to a downtown hotdog stand for a quick bite. We both ordered a Coney Island with a side order of cheesy, onion-topped chili. We gobbled up our greasy feast then walked the rest of the way to the theatre. The inside of the movie house was cavernous, with dim chandeliers hanging from a soaring high ceiling. A red, flood-lit curtain was pulled across the huge screen in front of us. We chatted for a bit, then the lights dimmed, the curtain parted, and the film began to roll.

The movie was dark, and riveting. Lana Turner betrayed her husband, and took up with a drifter. She was hatching a plot to have her poor husband murdered, when I felt the first waves of nausea. It got worse; I was going to throw up and there was nothing I could do to stop it. I puked into my purse; it was the best idea I could come up with. Folks around me whispered; I was really embarrassed, but confounded by how quickly the nausea passed. My friend whispered would I like to leave? I assured her that I felt fine, and went on with the movie. My aim was true; the mess had been completely contained to my purse. My compact, comb, and coin purse were now awash in a pond of vomit. I could take care of that later.

Ernie picked us up in front of the theatre after the show. We dropped my friend off then stopped to pick up a bag of White Castles for Florence. I yammered on about the movie; Ernie lit another cigarette and listened intently all the way home. Around the kitchen table, I resumed my critique of *The Postman Always Rings Twice* for Florence, who was gobbling up her little hamburgers. I told the story up to the point where Frank saved the pregnant Cora from suicide by drowning, thus stoking the dying embers of their adulterous love affair. I left out the part about Cora dying a short time later, and Frank being executed for her murder; I didn't want to go to bed on a bad note.

I awoke in the loft early the next morning. I was sick again. The bathroom was downstairs; my need was immediate. I jumped out of bed and looked around in the darkness for a container to vomit in. The only light in the room came from a floor vent that opened above the kitchen where a night light was always left on. I started in that direction when a tidal wave of nausea brought everything up; I bent over the floor vent and heaved. When it was all over, I peered through the vent grating at the kitchen table directly below. Flecks of hotdog skin and cheesy chili floated in a splatter of puke on the table top. I stood bolt upright; I now knew for sure I was pregnant. I had been suspicious; there had been other recent signs. I would make an appointment in the morning to see a doctor for confirmation.

I hurried downstairs to clean up the mess I'd made. Florence was a light sleeper. She heard the commotion in the kitchen and came to see what the fuss was all about. I filled her in, and a hushed celebration ensued. Just after daybreak, Florence got busy calling the other family members who had phones. It took several days for the baby news to reach the last of the family down south. I waited to tell Kenny until the pregnancy was confirmed by a doctor. As soon as I got the good news, I went downtown to Western Union and sent a telegram to Kenny's unit in Antwerp. It took two days for the telegram to reach Kenny in the field. I got a telegram back about a week later: Kenny had requested a furlough to coincide with my expected due date; his request was denied. We were all disappointed by the denial, but none more than Cammie Phillips. Not allowing a man to be with his wife for the birth of their first child was an insensitive travesty; unsatisfactory and unacceptable.

Kenny began getting regular letters from his Mom telling him to get home for the birth of his first child; to take matters into his own hands if need be. Cammie Phillips had never been in the military, of course, and didn't realize that this was not a job where you could simply turn in a resignation, and leave. A Private First Class did not negotiate with superiors; he saluted smartly, and did as he was told. In Belgium, the letters from Deputy continued to pour in. A few months later, on a rainy Friday night in Antwerp, the news of the arrival of a healthy baby boy reached Kenny. An hour later, his bags were packed. He wouldn't be missed until Monday morning's formation. He was going home.

Private First Class Kenny Phillips in Belgium, 1947

Antwerp was a bustling seaport. Cargo ships carrying occupation food and building supplies arrived daily from the States. After a short layover, the ships returned to one of several US port cities to reload, and return. Kenny made his way to the waterfront, and boarded the first ship he saw. He found a warm hiding place in the bowels of the freighter, and hunkered down. Although he didn't know it at the time, the ship was bound for the port of New Orleans. The crossing took nearly three weeks. Kenny soon discovered that he could move freely about the vessel in the wee hours of the morning. For a couple of hours each day he could visit the head, get drinking water, and steal fruit and canned goods from the galley. Upon arrival in New Orleans, he turned up the collar on his pea coat, donned his knitted watch cap, and slipped off the ship unnoticed. He had eight hundred miles to go to get to Indianapolis. Kenny changed back into his Army uniform, and thumbed a ride north. He had no trouble hitching rides; grateful civilians were quick to come to the aid of servicemen in uniform. Two days after leaving New Orleans, he arrived at the house on North Colorado with a knock on the kitchen door.

Stevie Edward Phillips, 1947

Kenny had been declared Absent Without Official Leave (AWOL) several days after leaving Antwerp. The Army had my official residence address in Indianapolis, and would probably be looking for their AWOL soldier there first. We made the decision to hide out in Paris Crossing. The following day, Ernie drove us downstate in his smoke-filled Buick. Mom and Dad took us in, and so began our life on the lam. We soon settled into a routine; Kenny helped Dad with the crops, while I took over care of the animals, collected eggs, and milked the cows. Small game was still abundant, and I resumed my childhood duties of bringing home an occasional rabbit or squirrel. This time, I used Jay's ancient .22 rifle instead of snares. I introduced Kenny and Stevie to the magical Turtle Pond. We went there to picnic, catch fish, and enjoy the abundance of wildlife that lived there.

Our last Sunday outing to the Turtle Pond was especially memorable; we were treated to a visit by a family of raccoons. A mom with four kits appeared out of the bushes directly across the pond. She didn't see us sitting quietly in the shade of a bankside sycamore. The little bandit-faced kits batted at mom's bushy tail as she crouched down for a drink of water. Stevie couldn't contain his delight; he squealed aloud. Mother raccoon was startled; she struck a menacing pose, emitted a low growl, and retreated back into the bushes with kits in tow. Before heading home, we gathered a bucket of pawpaw fruit that I would use to make an ice cream-like dessert for an evening treat. With the sun getting low in the western sky, we started our walk home along the railroad tracks. It was a beautiful evening: Clouds under lit by the setting sun took on the color of apricots; the air was still and warm. It was a perfect end to a perfect day.

We rounded the bend in the tracks and saw some kind of commotion in the distance. On the slope in front of the farmhouse, Mom and Dad were having what appeared to be an animated argument with a group of men. As we drew closer, Kenny realized what was going on. The men at the farmhouse wore Army uniforms; they had come for him. They spotted us, and began walking our way. We picked up the pace and met them half way. Kenny was immediately taken into custody, and marched down the tracks to Paris Crossing. Waiting there was an olive drab sedan with an Army insignia on the door. They put Kenny in the back seat with an MP on either side, and drove off into the setting sun. It was several days before we got word that Kenny had been sent back to Europe to complete his service obligation. Due to the circumstances of his misbehavior, someone in the chain of command made the compassionate decision to go light on him. The outcome could have been much worse.

I carried on at home in Paris Crossing; I helped with the farm chores, and the parents helped me with Stevie. It was nearly a year later that Kenny wrote to say he was finally being sent home to process out at Fort Bragg, North Carolina. Kenny had already secured military housing for us at Fort Bragg. Soon, we were packed up and on our way to the train station, and the next chapter in our adventure.

Waiting for the train to Fayetteville

The first leg of our train trip was pretty exciting for Stevie. He stood on his seat with his nose pressed against the window as North Vernon slipped out of view. There was an elderly couple sitting across from us. They introduced themselves as the Coltons, and explained that they were on their way to a new life in Florida. The couple had owned and operated a neighborhood restaurant in Minneapolis for thirty-seven years. They had never experienced a winter without freezing temperatures and snow. They were looking forward to spending their twilight years on the warm sand of a Florida beach. They had sold the restaurant for a good price, and were now on the way to live their dream.

Mrs. Colton carried a wicker picnic basket on her lap. She opened the lid and pulled out a fresh oatmeal cookie, passed the basket over to her husband, and invited Stevie to come sit with her. The cookie bait worked like magic; Stevie rode the rest of the way to Cincinnati on Mrs. Colton's lap, eating cookies and listening to stories about her grandchildren his age back in Minnesota. Our train pulled into the Cincinnati station late in the afternoon. I compared notes with the Coltons; we both needed to board a different train for the journey south. The new train was on the opposite side of the railyard. I grabbed our luggage and Stevie, and went into the station to find a phone booth. I called the Dodd Funeral Home and asked that they pass word to Mom and Dad that we were doing fine, and I would call again once we got settled in Fayetteville. We went to the other side of the railyard and found our train, turned over our tickets, and boarded a car just like the one that brought us to Cincinnati.

After we were seated and our luggage stowed, I stood up in the aisle and looked around for the Coltons; I didn't see them. I figured they had been assigned another car. Both

Stevie and I had taken quite a shine to the old couple, and I intended to buy them dinner that evening. I asked the next porter to come by which car they might be on; he asked me to describe them, and I did. "Oh" he replied; "They're in the Colored Car." And so I learned something new: Trains headed south out of Ohio had a special car for the colored folks. It seemed silly; the same people we rode with on our train car out of North Vernon were now segregated into two groups and sent to different cars.

I grabbed Stevie and took off to find the Coltons. We found the Colored Car and went in. My first impression was that the car looked cluttered. Passengers sat with their belongings piled up around their feet; there were no overhead storage bins. At the car's entrance was a single bathroom for the men and women to share. Every eye followed us as we walked down the aisle. We found our friends seated in the middle of the car, undeterred and cheerful to see us. Mr. Colton saw my puzzled look and shrugged, as if to say; "don't worry, ain't nothing… we're used to this".

I announced that Stevie and I had come to fetch them for dinner in the dining car. An awkward silence followed. I learned my second lesson for the day: Coloreds were not allowed in the dining car, thus the wicker picnic basket Mrs. Colton was carrying. I glanced around at the other passengers; they all had picnic baskets, or tote bags, carrying the food they needed for their trip. There was plenty of food I was told. We were invited to sit and eat; I gladly accepted. From the wicker basket, Mrs. Colton produced thick ham sandwiches wrapped in wax paper. Several ladies from the back of the car came forward to make over Stevie. We ate our fill and chattered about this and that until it was time to leave. We bade the Coltons farewell, and returned to the White Car for the night.

Our train pulled into the Fayetteville station, on a cold, blustery, morning. I had called Kenny from the North Vernon station before leaving Indiana. He would be on duty when we were scheduled to arrive, and was sending the girlfriend of an Army buddy to pick us up. She went by the name of Mel. We found Mel in the station holding a piece of cardboard with my name scrawled on it. She wore a heavy wool coat over a worn bathrobe; she had fuzzy slippers on her feet, and her hair was a tangled mess. She babbled nonstop from the time we left the train station about a recent life-changing event.

It seems she had become host to an enormous parasitic worm. For months, she had inexplicably lost weight, while growing what appeared to be a beer belly. She felt fine in spite of this, so didn't seek medical attention. The culprit finally came to light at a dinner party hosted by her husband's Commanding Officer. As she told it, someone at the table cracked a joke just as she was about to take a bite of buttery mashed potato. Pausing to laugh, the forkful of food hovered just outside her mouth for a moment. Those looking in her direction were horrified to see a slender blue worm dart out of her wide-open mouth, strike at the ball of mashed potato like a snake, grab off a bite, and snap quickly back into its lair. The sight touched off a panic; the hostess fainted, women screamed and glasses broke as the diners instinctively recoiled in horror.

Mel was taking medicine to kill the invader. Every day new segments up to a foot long would pass out in her stool. The expelled worm segments were not quite dead yet. If Mel stayed too long on the toilet, they would start inching up the porcelain toilet bowl, trying in vain to return home.

I was on the verge of puking when Mel pulled up in front of our duplex. A civilian facilities guy was waiting for us. He had turned on the gas and lit the pilot lights. I was given a tour of the house, and a map showing where everything was at Fort Bragg. I signed for the keys, and began unpacking. Through the window I saw an Army vehicle pull up in front of the house; it was Kenny. The timing was perfect; Stevie was down for a nap.

After a wonderful hour of reconnecting, we sat in the kitchen dining nook to get caught up. First and foremost, I wanted to know why he sent a raving lunatic to pick us up. Kenny acted surprised and shocked; he leaned forward as I retold the story of the dinner worm. I was only half way through the story when Kenny lost control; he burst out laughing. I knew immediately I'd been had; he was, after all, one of the notorious Phillips boys. Mel was the girlfriend of Spuz, an Army buddy he met in Antwerp. The three of them concocted the story, and Mel pulled it off perfectly.

Our time at Fort Bragg was one big party. The war was over, the men were processing out, and jobs were plentiful. We were all so young. Nearly half the couples had a young child like us, the rest were doing their best to catch up. I know this for a fact; the walls in military housing were paper thin, leaving very little to the imagination. I was there for the start of the Baby Boom; I heard it unfolding first-hand. It was a very social scene. We frequently dined together, or met up for a night playing cards, drinking beer, and telling war stories. The ladies normally abstained from drinking, knowing that any one of us could be early pregnant. It didn't matter; we were having the time of our lives, and a promising future lay before us.

Kenny had become buddies with two southern boys while stationed in Belgium. Rodney Mullis was from the hollows of West Virginia. He was a true hillbilly, as was his wife. I had heard the word "hillbilly" used by Hoosiers to jokingly disparage anyone from Kentucky, but I had never met a hillbilly in person until the Mullis couple moved into the other half of our duplex. Maxwell Maple was a tall, lanky kid from Warner Robbins, Georgia. Max had earned the nickname "Spuz" for reasons unknown. Mel was his girlfriend. He was carefree, goofy, and chain-smoked cigars. All three young men were pranksters. They had been disciplined in Belgium for stealing an outhouse.

Kenny, Rodney, and Spuz (seated) Antwerp, 1946

It was never their intention to steal the outhouse; just relocate it from over the septic pit. They knew the owner would need to go pee on that moonless night, stumble across the back yard, and hopefully do a face plant into the chasm and its vile pudding. This was payback in a running game of one-upmanship with the outhouse owner, himself a prankster. This had started a week earlier. The men were drinking together in an Antwerp public house when there was a falling out of some sort. Kenny and his buddies left the tavern a short while later. They were unable to start their Army vehicle for the trip back to the base. The Jeep wouldn't start because a large potato had been pounded into the tailpipe. It was two in the morning, sleeting, and they were five miles from their base. They took off walking, arriving back at the barracks at dawn; just in time to clean up, and make morning formation. In front of the whole platoon, the perpetrator made the unwise decision to take full, gloating, ownership of the cause for their night of misery. Now he would pay dearly.

We became good friends with our next door neighbors, Rodney and Mary Mullis. They were wonderful, fun-loving folks. Rodney had never slept between sheets before entering the Army. It was the first time in his life he had to wear shoes. Chipped beef on toast, or Shit On a Shingle (SOS) was an Army chow hall standard. Rodney confided that SOS was the most delicious dish he had ever eaten. When the day came for them to go home to West Virginia, I prepared a farewell meal of fancied-up Shit On a Shingle to die for. Spuz and Mel showed up for after-dinner beer and cigars. Spuz would also be leaving for home in the morning, taking Mel with him. The army buddies drank beer and recounted their European capers until the wee hours of the morning. Just before daybreak, we all exchanged teary hugs, and vowed to stay in touch, which we never did. Kenny was discharged two weeks later. We packed our bags and boarded the White Car bound for Indiana, by way of Cincinnati.

7 THE END OF AN ERA

The Law family had been in Paris Crossing nearly as long as the Humphreys. Rupert Law was a boy a few years older than I. He had been injured in a freak accident, and was not quite right in the head. Rupert was helping his father dig a well several years back, when a big rock fell some twenty feet and hit him square on top of the head. Mom and Dad instructed us be kind to Rupert, who was left simple and spastic by the tragic accident.

At first, Rupert was as excited about the new rink as the rest of us kids, but roller skating proved to be very difficult for him. Rupert could generate great speed, but couldn't negotiate the turns at each end of the long straightaway. He repeatedly smashed hard into the low wooden walls that ringed the hardwood floor. Some of the older boys were mean to Rupert; they found his clumsy misfortunes hilarious. To make matters worse, Rupert's mother insisted he wear a ridiculous tattered old football helmet for protection. I'm ashamed to say that a few of the Paris Crossing girls joined in. Mocking and teasing Rupert became a mean spirited feature of Saturday skate night. After several weeks of humiliation, Rupert quit trying. We never saw him inside the rink again. Instead, he spent his Saturday nights across the street in front of Humphrey's Cash Store; he sat on a produce crate, listening to the old men's stories, chewing Mail Pouch tobacco, and glowering in silence at the rink.

The day before we left Fayetteville, I got a disturbing letter from Mom. She brought the terrible news that the south side of Main Street had burned to the ground, and Rupert was in jail. Rupert had taken to heavy drinking. Townsfolk familiar with his tragic life story tolerated his public drunkenness, as did the local constable who was a distant relative of the Law family. I suspected the pain and humiliation of those Saturday nights at the rink were responsible for Rupert giving up, and descending into a life of alcoholism.

Something finally snapped, and on a humid summer night, Rupert rose from his produce crate in front of the store. He staggered across the street with a jerry can full of gasoline. He doused the rink, and set it ablaze. The fire quickly spread to the post office next door, and then to the gas station and garage on the corner. The entire south side of Main Street was consumed by the blaze. The volunteer fire fighters were unable to approach the roaring blaze; they could do nothing but stand back and watch it burn. Neither the rink, nor any of the other buildings destroyed by the fire were ever rebuilt. A new post office opened in a trailer that occupied the lot where the rink had sat. Rupert Law was eventually convicted of arson and sent to prison.

The great fire came at a time of general decline in the rural villages as we had known them. In the years following my move to the city, everything began to unravel in the little farming towns. With fewer children, schools were closed and consolidated. With the passing of our elders, and with no one to carry on, farms ceased to produce, and fell into disrepair. The main street merchants were the next to go, resulting in relative ghost towns that once bustled with vibrant activity. The land was cheap, and soon was being bought up by folks from the city. Government controls on development had never been seen as necessary up to that time. Before long, a hodgepodge of tacky structures began to spring up on the most accessible parcels, usually along the two-lane highways that connected the towns. Large tracts of hardwood forest were cleared, demands on groundwater increased with each new well, and the native fish and wildlife that had sustained us for decades, began to disappear.

In Paris Crossing, the Dodd Funeral Home ceased operations about this time. The magnificent brick mansion that had once been the finest home on Main Street began to fall into disrepair. The new generation of Dodd children had moved away, leaving no one to carry on the family business. Cora, the matriarch of the Dodd clan, spent her final years on the expansive front porch, waving to passers-by, and shooting the breeze with anyone who had time to sit a spell. After her passing, the old mansion fell into ruin, and was eventually demolished. The rubble from the old mansion remains scattered about the property to this day, barely visible through the tangle of weeds, bushes and vines that are gradually reclaiming the land.

Humphrey's Cash Store was founded by my Great Grandfather, Gaston Humphrey, in 1865. My cousin Briz was the last Humphrey to own and operate the store. After a century of family ownership, the store was sold to another local family. A fire of suspicious origin broke out shortly thereafter. The store burned to the ground, taking the farm supplies building too, and causing great damage to the rebuilt post office on the other side of Main Street. Falling student enrollments brought about school consolidations that closed the Paris Crossings School. The elementary grades were bussed to Graham Elementary, and the high schoolers to Deputy. Efforts to keep the historic Paris school building failed. The architectural masterpiece was demolished, and replaced with a windowless, steel warehouse. The final blow to the Paris Crossing I knew came when the trains stopped running. The Baltimore & Ohio railroad from North Vernon to Louisville had been vital to the town of Paris Crossing for decades.

Farming had been a way of life that had persisted for hundreds of years, but all of this changed during my lifetime. My generation was the first to leave the country for jobs in the city. We left our subsistence economy, for a money economy: we no longer provided for ourselves, but spent our wages buying the necessities of life with money. In turn, we now devoted our life energy to making this-or-that to sell to others.

Everywhere, it seemed, this migration to the city was occurring. We were seeking a "better life," and in most ways we achieved what we considered a higher standard of living. The thought never occurred to us at the time, but the price of this transformation was total dependence on people and events beyond our control.

To be sure, there were lots of positives too. Life in the city was much, much easier: we worked fewer, less laborious hours. We had a bathroom with running water, and an indoor toilet. We could now take care of our personal business without the ghastly odor of the summer outhouse, or the visually obscene winter chamber pots. The house was heated by an oil furnace in the floor; no more need to saw wood and gather coal to feed the pot belly stove. The ice box was replaced with a more efficient electric refrigerator. In the fridge was an assortment of store-bought food; not as fresh, nor delicious as farm food, but it had already been killed, or picked, and cleaned; all we had to do was cook it.

"City Slicker" was a derisive label us country folks applied to the well-dressed hustlers that occasionally came through Paris Crossing, usually selling something. When we settled in Columbus, we found most of the folks were just like us; hard-working young couples recently resettled from the country, come to the city for a better life. Unlike the farm, however, the city offered some very creative ways to make money without producing anything of real value. In a money economy, there was lots of room for shenanigans; cleverness and deceit could be rewarded handsomely. These attributes were worthless on the farm, where hard work was rewarded, and trickery got you nothing but the scorn of your neighbors.

8 COLUMBUS

There was a story that Daddy used to tell that had been passed down through the years. My Grandfather, Larkin Cook, was a member of the Independent Order of Odd Fellows, a charitable fraternity similar to the Freemasons. Shortly before his untimely death, Grandpa Larkin took Daddy and his older brother Charles to the 1898 Odd Fellows family reunion in Indianapolis. A circus tent was erected to provide the kids a safe place to play during the day while the adults conducted Lodge business.

Grandpa Larkin was taking the boys to their dormitory when a woman shouted for help. She complained that a kid was inside the tent, walking under the bleachers tying to see up women's dresses. Charles and Jessie were sent under the bleachers to investigate. They found a bespectacled twelve year old boy, intently studying the steel bracing that held the wooden benches aloft. He was making pencil notes on a pad of scratch paper. The boy glanced at Daddy and Charles, and continued sketching. Then he offered an explanation without looking up from his work: "I'm building a steam motorcar. I've got the motor started, and now I need to build the frame; I'm learning a lot under here."

Daddy and Charles came out from under the bleachers choking back laughter, and reported their findings to their father: There was a boy under there, but he was not looking up anyone's dress; he was studying the steel bracing for his steam motorcar. Father Larkin smiled knowingly; "Oh hell that's Clessie Cummins." Grandpa Larkin confirmed that Clessie was indeed building a steam engine in his father's barn; his inventive intelligence was legendary among the Lodgers and the folks of Henry County where the Cummins family lived. His brilliance was the creative force behind the Cummins Diesel Company. The company he founded in 1919 prospered, and became internationally known for quality diesel motors. By the time we arrived, Cummins was by far the biggest employer in Columbus.

Post-war Columbus was booming. Cummins was hiring qualified veterans for entry level positions. Arvin, the company I had worked for in Indianapolis, had just opened a new factory and was hiring assemblers. I went for an interview, and was hired on the spot. Kenny hoped to be hired as an apprentice in one of Cummins' machine shops. There was a flood of men coming out of the military at that time, and many of them had better qualifications. After a short period of unemployment, Kenny answered an advertisement seeking a managing partner for a neighborhood grocery store. The following day he reported for work at the Cherry Street Grocery to learn the ins and outs of being a grocer. We rented a little white cottage on Cherry Street two blocks from the store. Here, we settled in as a family for the first time.

At Arvin, I picked up where I left off, working on an assembly line making household appliances. Kenny was learning to operate a cash register, stock shelves, prepare purchase orders, and deal with customers of all stripes. Stevie was cared for by Mrs. Walker, an elderly neighbor who ran a daycare service out of her home. Stevie wasn't at all happy with the new arrangement. We knew Mrs. Walker was a spinster cat lady, and a little quirky. Her house reeked of cat urine. Kenny and I had no child care alternative at the time, so we chose to overlook her untidy ways. It was only a temporary arrangement, and it was important that both Kenny and I worked. Stevie was a trooper; he never complained beyond letting us know he didn't like going there. We learned months later that Mrs. Walker fed the kids concentration camp food; a lunch of watery potato soup and a single slice of white bread every day, five days a week. Stevie was frightened by her appearance. She wore the same housecoat every day; her hair was usually up in curlers and covered by a scarf. Mrs. Walker was fascinated by UFOs. She often lectured the kids on the existence of flying saucers and aliens that lived among us undetected.

We were soon earning money that covered our needs, and then some. We used our new-found wealth to buy our first car; a 1950 Chevy Convertible Coupe. Next, we bought our first television: a big-cabinet RCA with a little fuzzy screen. We had our choice of two television channels, plus a third bonus channel when the weather conditions were just so. Our first family television viewing experience was an episode of Buffalo Bob's Howdy Doody Show.

We began dining out for the first time. With both of us working, it made sense to pay someone else to do the cooking once or twice a week. Our favorite restaurant in Columbus was the Palms Café on Fourth Street. For a couple of farm kids, this was elegant dining. The menu selections were delicious and varied. The café atmosphere and décor were inviting. Tommy Dorsey, Benny Goodman, and Glen Miller music playing throughout the restaurant rounded out the experience.

Sisters Genevieve and Alice had settled in nearby Bethel Village, a suburban community of new homes five miles southwest of Columbus. Alice was married to Leland Cochran, a quiet, handsome man from Deputy. Lee and

Alice had three sons, all close to Stevie's age. Genevieve lived two blocks away with daughter Joan, and husband Hubert. We all saw a lot of each other during our time together in Columbus. Summer picnics at Brown County State Park, or Donner Park in Columbus, brought the whole family together again. The kids played and swam together, and took turns sitting on Uncle Hube's ice cream maker while he turned the crank. The men played shuffleboard, tossed horseshoes, and talked about fishing and cars. We sisters effortlessly revived our sibling rivalry, and soon were arguing about everything again like we'd never been apart.

It was a well-known fact that Stevie could identify every car on the road from an early age. How he got this knowledge was a total mystery. My Dad loved his grandson, but thought Stevie was a freak of nature, and encouraged me to enjoy him while I could, because "children like him never live very long." At the family picnics, the men sometimes engaged in a game of "Stump Stevie." They would take their lawn chairs to the edge of the road that ran through the park, then take turns pointing out cars for Stevie to identify. No one was ever able to stump him.

There was an exceptionally rare automobile parked in a driveway close to Donner Park. It was an expensive luxury car made in a factory in Connersville, Indiana. Uncle Hube found out about the car, and decided to put Stevie to the ultimate test. At the next Donner Park picnic, Kenny and Hube grabbed Stevie, and piled into Ernie's smoke-filled Buick. The men returned ten minutes later. Stevie ran off to join his cousins at the play area. The men approached the picnic bench shaking their heads in disbelief; Stevie had correctly identified the 1929 Cord, right down to the model number.

1929 Cord L-29

The Columbus city schools required new students to be of age by the beginning of the school year in August. That created a problem, as Stevie would not be of age until November. Back in Paris Crossing, the school district admitted new students who came of age by the end of the calendar year. Stevie was a bright boy and was ready for school. Neither Kenny nor I wanted him held back.

I talked it over with my parents. They agreed to let Stevie come and live with them for his first year of school. We changed his residence to Paris Crossing in August, got him enrolled, and moved him down to the farm in time for the first day of classes. I'm not sure Stevie cared for the move at first, but quickly got used to it. We sweetened the pot somewhat with the gift of a dog; a golden cocker spaniel he named Nippy. Soon after Stevie's arrival on the farm, he was befriended by an alpha goose, a direct descendant of Jay's Matilda. Stevie named the goose Wilmer. The threesome spent hours exploring the gallery woods along the stream that ran through the Cook's pasture; Nippy in the lead, followed by Stevie, with waddling Wilmer bringing up the rear.

Stevie and Wilmer

Kenny and I missed having our son under the same roof, but at the same time were glad to have a few months alone to work on our marriage. Cracks had started to appear in our foundation; we were arguing daily, about every little thing. We both tried to make it work. Stevie had witnessed the beginning of this, and became deeply, visibly, upset every time our raised voices escalated to an angry acting out of some sort.

The worst of these episodes happened on a Friday night, on our way to Paris Crossing. The argument started the moment we pulled away from the curb in Columbus. The argument increased in intensity, eventually becoming a physical fight in North Vernon. Stevie sobbed in the back seat as we exchanged punches and pulled each other's hair. In a theatrical show of anger, Kenny drove to the steps of the North Vernon courthouse where we were married, got out of the car, and demanded a divorce. It was a dark night. When Kenny opened the passenger door to drag me out, the dome light came on. My face was covered with blood; something Stevie had never seen; he screamed and burst into tears. His pitiful pleading put an end to the episode. We rode in stomach-churning silence the rest of the way to the Paris Crossing turnoff. Kenny pulled over, kicked us out of the car, and sped off to Deputy.

We walked the mile or so from the highway to town, then down the railroad tracks to the house. Dad opened the door. He stood silent for a moment staring at my blood-caked face. I had also bled all over Stevie, who I had to carry up the tracks the last hundred yards or so. Without a word, Dad ushered us inside and called out for Mom. Dad went into his bedroom, emerged with a loaded 12 gauge shotgun, and went off into the night to find and kill Kenny.

Fortunately for all involved, Kenny was safe at the Phillips farm in Deputy; getting an angry earful from mother Cammie. When Dad failed to find Kenny in Paris Crossing, he returned to the house, quietly unloaded the shotgun, put it back behind the bedroom door, and came over to comfort Stevie. In all the years before or since, I never saw him as angry as he was that night. Meanwhile, over in Deputy, Kenny was getting the verbal thrashing of his life. Gene and Cammie Phillips taught their boys to never strike anyone in anger, and never hit a woman for any reason. Kenny was told in no uncertain terms, that he would go to Paris Crossing in the morning and make this ugly situation right.

I awoke the following morning with my face stuck to the pillow. Mom had applied Mercurochrome to the cuts on my face the night before. I went to the dresser and picked up a hand mirror; my face was a frightening mess of scabs and red Mercurochrome stains. I got dressed and went to the kitchen where Stevie was having breakfast with my parents;

he started crying when he saw my face. The shocking sight re-ignited Dad's rage, and brought renewed promises to put a load of buckshot into Kenny's "cowardly ass." Then there came a knock at the front door.

Dad opened the door. There stood Kenny, head bowed, looking frightened and contrite. I noticed with unexpected pleasure that I had given a pretty good accounting of myself in the fight; Kenny's right eye was swollen shut, and blackened. I had landed a blow to the mouth that cut his lower lip. It was swollen. Dad lunged through the door and grabbed Kenny by the neck. He pulled his fist back to strike a blow, and then let him go. Kenny burst into tears; I quickly followed. We embraced we forgave, and vowed that this would never happen again. Our thoughts quickly turned to Stevie who was taking this all in with an emotionless stare, tears running down his cheeks. He had been shaken to the core. We could forgive and forget and move on; Stevie could not. He had been scarred for life, and there was nothing we could ever do to change that.

The following Sunday, Kenny and I attended the Columbus Methodist Church for the first time. We got a warm reception from the congregation; it felt like home. We needed this in our lives just then; putting God at the head of or our family would save our rocky marriage, we hoped. We joined the church, and sang in the choir. Every week we attended Sunday school before the morning service. Choir practice was held in the church basement on Tuesday evenings. We were back on Wednesday night for Prayer Meeting. I connected immediately with the teachings of Christ. I had experienced the life-saving grace of the Holy Spirit when we buried Jay, and again on the Thanksgiving when Willa Jane locked me in the steamer trunk. Kenny and I quit fighting altogether. We rarely argued aloud about anything, and agreed to never act out in front of Stevie. Ours was a happy home again. It was a time of healing for our marriage, but Stevie had stopped smiling… he was still reeling from the night at the North Vernon courthouse. There was a fruit tree in our backyard. Stevie went to climb up and sit in the tree every day now, alone with his thoughts.

One blustery afternoon in February, a talkative young guy happened into the Cherry Street Grocery. He had just returned home to Columbus from a stint in the Navy. The sailor had spent most of his tour assigned to an aircraft carrier home ported in San Diego. He described California as the Promised Land: There were good jobs to be had, it was an endless summer without seasons, the fishing was out of this world, and all the women were tanned and beautiful.

It was cold and rainy outside, and business was slow. Kenny and Roy invited the young sailor to have a seat by the pot belly stove, and tell them more. The sailor was headed back to California to start an apprenticeship with Ryan Aeronautical, based in San Diego. The sailor mentioned that it was Ryan that built the Spirit of Saint Louis for Charles Lindbergh for his trans-Atlantic hop in 1927. All of the West Coast aircraft factories that beefed up to turn out bombers and fighters for the War were now being flooded with new peacetime contracts. Many companies were hiring for entry level training programs that paid a good living wage. The trainees were taught the skills that would lead to careers as machinists, technicians, and quality control experts.

Kenny came home from the store that evening with California on his mind. It was all he could talk about. I had not seen him this excited since Fayetteville, on the day he was discharged from the Army. We sat at the kitchen table and talked until the wee hours of the morning. It was a frightening prospect: leaving our parents, siblings, cousins, and life-long friends, to move two thousand miles away to a land where we didn't know a soul; a place very different from Indiana. On the other hand, this could be the adventure of a lifetime. We were young; both just shy of twenty-five. If things didn't work out in California, we could return home to our loved ones, and carry on with life. The time we had taken to work on our marriage had yielded positive results; there had been no more physical violence since the ugly scene at the North Vernon courthouse. California would be a fresh start, a new beginning away from the influence of kinfolk, an adventure shared. By dawn, the watershed decision was made; we were moving to California.

Kenny left for work a few hours later. At the store, a red-eyed Roy related a similar scene that had played out in Roy's home with his wife, Evelyn. They too had made the decision to go. Roy and Evelyn were three years older than us, and had a daughter, Lottie, with special medical needs. Their daughter's future played a big role in their decision. The hospitals and clinics in Los Angeles held the promise of a cure for her condition. The men began spending as much time as the business would allow planning the trip. There was a lot to do: The store would need to be sold, notifications made, expenses estimated, and enough money squirreled away to pay trip expenses, and endure a month or two of unemployment once we reached California. It was February; all of this would take some time, at least six months by our estimate. The first day of July was circled on the calendar as our planned departure date.

9 ROUTE 66

The Cherry Street Grocery sold quickly. Roy and Kenny agreed to provide two months of assistance and training for the new owners; a local family that was relocating to the city from a farm near Madison. This insured we would have an income right up to the day of our departure. We began spending as much time as we could with our parents in Paris Crossing, and Deputy. We had to turn in our keys to the house on Cherry Street the last week in June. Hube and Ginny agreed to take us in for our final nights in Columbus. Everything was coming together nicely.

I barely knew Roy, and had never met his wife. It was important to me that we all get to know each other better before hitting the road. Kenny and I thought it would be fun to take them out for a casual evening at the Palms Café on Fourth Street. Kenny took our proposal to Roy at the store the next day. It turned out that the Palms was also their favorite place for a sit down dinner. We made a date for the following Saturday. We needed a babysitter to watch over Stevie. My sisters would gladly take him for the evening, but Bethel Village was too long a drive. We settled on Roy's neighbors who regularly babysat Lottie, their daughter. It was after dark when we went to their house for the first time to drop off the kids.

The couple lived next door to Roy on a huge weed-covered lot. You couldn't see their house trailer from the street. We entered the yard by flashlight, through a rusty chain-link gate, and followed Roy down a dirt path that meandered toward some lights in the distance. On both sides of the path, heaps of junk rose above the waist-high weeds; a burst water heater, a couple of dead cars, a broken-down swing set. The path brought us to a single wide trailer that had slipped off its jacks long ago. Half of the trailer had stayed aloft on its piers, cracking the roof open when the other half fell. The roof was now covered with a heavy tarp, bricked down to keep the rain out. Roy rattled the aluminum door. We were greeted seconds later by Bonny, the lady of the house. She led us uphill, and into the living room where her husband Mack had just finished his supper of potato chips and Big Red soda. Bonny was a tall, noble looking woman; she had prominent cheek bones and an attractive overbite that suggested a Cherokee ancestor. Her long hair was black and worn straight.

Bonnie and Mack were unemployed chain smokers. They had two babies; identical twin girls. Bonny's sister was serving a prison sentence. Her nephew Carl had come to live with them until his mother's release; he was the same age as Stevie. We took a seat and spent some time getting to know them. If you overlooked their dreadful living conditions and personal habits, Bonnie and Mack appeared to be genuine people with generous hearts. They reminded me of the hillbilly Mullis couple we'd known from our time in Fayetteville, but more refined. By the time we got up to leave for dinner, I was comfortable with leaving Stevie in their care.

Roy was a big man with very little to say. He was polite, and generous. Evelyn was a blue-eyed blond, petite and cute. She wanted to be a movie star. Evelyn talked endlessly about celebrities; called them by their first name as if she knew them personally. Kenny was mesmerized by the little doll. Under the table, I rode herd on his fornicating grin with

painful kicks to the shin. Evelyn read the tabloids: We all
listened politely as she related the latest news about
Humphrey Bogart. Bogie had been diagnosed with a
terminal disease. The little pixie wept at the thought of what
Lauren must be going through. She hoped to find Lauren in
California, and comfort her. She had written a letter in care
of Lauren's studio to let her know she was coming. I
discreetly rolled my eyes and took the Lord's name in vain
under breath. In all fairness to the shallow tart, Bogie *did*
have a dread disease, and died from it a few years later.

Our waiter brought the check, and Roy snatched it up. On
top of paying for dinner, he called the wait staff over,
thanked them individually, and handed them a generous tip.
Roy was not a well man. Kenny told me that Roy had
volunteered for service after Pearl Harbor, but was turned
away because of a hereditary heart condition. It was the
main reason Roy had advertised for a partner in the little
grocery store; he had been ordered to avoid heavy lifting,
and to work fewer hours. Lottie, their daughter, had an
undiagnosed illness that had the couple going to an
Indianapolis specialist once a month in an effort to find out
why the little girl slept all the time and was not growing. In
light of this, I grudgingly gave tabloid Evelyn credit for
staying upbeat and taking care of her closest loved ones;
she was always positive and smiling. We left the restaurant
and headed home. We backtracked through the weedy
jungle, got the kids, and parted ways around midnight. I was
fine now with Roy and Evelyn as traveling partners: Roy was
an absolute prince, and Evelyn promised endless hours of
low comedy.

My precious Uncle Charlie was now living in the Odd Fellows
Home in Greensburg. His wife, Aunt Lizzie, died in her sleep

in their Madison home. She was preceded in death by her mother, who had lived with them for years. Charlie needed daily assistance now; he was admitted to the Odd Fellow's rest home to live out the remainder of his days. I went to Greensburg for one last visit. Genevieve drove. To our young noses, all old people emitted a distinct, medicinal odor. It wasn't pleasant, nor was it terribly bad, it just was. The imposing, stone, two-story Odd Fellow's building reeked of old people. We were directed to the second floor and Uncle Charlie's room. We hugged and cried; our visit was unannounced, our dear Uncle was surprised, and overwhelmed. All of the interior surfaces of the rest home were painted green. Charlie had a dresser, a desk and chair, and a bed. His one window overlooked a courtyard. Fox squirrels scampered up and down a huge Hickory tree that grew to within a few feet of his window. Ginny and I lost track of time. Parting was more difficult than usual this time; I loved him so.   I would be leaving for California in a few weeks, and very likely would never see my precious Uncle again.

 We got back to Columbus from Greensburg after dark. Kenny was waiting at home with some unexpected news; Bonny and Mack were coming with us to California. I took a seat in the kitchen breakfast nook, as Kenny explained: Mack had a brother in Los Angeles who co-founded a successful toy company in 1948. The fledgling enterprise took off like a rocket.   His brother had been trying for months to get him out West to no avail. Mack was an unemployed woodworker; his skills were needed to perfect a new product the company had on the drawing board. It seems that our excitement had worn off on Bonny and Mack; they talked it over, and decided going west in a caravan of friends would be better than going it alone at some later date. Bonnie's family owned the lot and house trailer in Columbus, and they had accumulated very few belongings. Pulling up stakes in Columbus would be a breeze. Mack had a job waiting for him in LA. His challenge would be helping to perfect a cost-effective way to fabricate and produce symmetrical wooden hoops. The new toy was going to be marketed as suitable for young and old; fun for the kids and great exercise for adults. They had dreamed up a marketing angle using a Hawaiian theme; the new product would be called a Hula Hoop, due to the users' gyrations mimicking those of a Waikiki Hula dancer.

Our last day on Cherry Street came quickly. We spent the day cleaning and packing, and saying goodbye to neighbors. We arrived at Hube and Ginny's home in Bethel Village with our meager worldly belongings stuffed into the trunk of the convertible. Stevie would ride in the rear seat, along with our food supply, drinking water, and clothes. At first light on the morning of July first, we left Hube and Ginny's house in Bethel Village to rendezvous with the others at the Columbus Methodist Church parking lot.

We found Mack and his family waiting for us in their rusty Plymouth station wagon. Bonnie was changing one of the twins on the hood of the car; a cigarette dangled from the corner of her mouth. Mack had just finished his breakfast of potato chips and Big Red. He emerged from the car, slapped the crumbs off his stained undershirt, and belched. He took a Pall Mall from Bonnie's crumpled pack, acknowledged us with a wave, and lit up. The roof of the station wagon was piled high with belongings, tarped over, and tied down with several mismatched hanks of rope. A trickle of some unknown fluid flowed from beneath the Plymouth and formed a pool below the radiator. The whole station wagon seemed to lean to the left a bit. Through the grimy backseat window I caught a glimpse of their nephew Carl digging out a difficult booger. "La Cucaracha" heralded the arrival of Roy and Evelyn. The novelty horn was a present from Evelyn, who had it installed in Roy's Oldsmobile for his last birthday. Evelyn emerged theatrically from the Olds, and started into a hokey interpretation of the Mexican Hat Dance; she wore huge sunglasses, a straw hat she'd combed into a sombrero, tight white pedal pushers, and stiletto heels.

The men unfolded a map on the hood of the Chevy, and huddled to run through last-minute details. They had spent a lot of time preparing for what lay ahead; we had all purchased heavy canvas water bags for the inevitable over-heating that was a standard feature of cars at that time. The bags hung from short lengths of rope slung over the hood ornaments. Air conditioners of the day were window mounted and looked similar to a tubular floor vacuum. Roy had purchased a brand a new unit for the Oldsmobile. We had the only convertible in the group, and thought naively that we could just drop the top if it got too hot. The plan was to keep each other in sight on the road. The men agreed on rendezvous points along the way in case we lost track of each other. Our destination on the first day was Joplin, Missouri. We figured it would take about nine hours to cover the 560 miles from Columbus to Joplin. That would get us there with a couple of hours of daylight left to find a place to stay the night.

The caravan pulled out of the Methodist Church parking lot with our Chevy in the lead. We drove southwest, and crossed the Wabash River into Illinois at Vincennes. Soon we were sailing through the endless cornfields of southern

Illinois. We stopped at a roadside park in the little town of Carlisle for a picnic lunch, then back on the road. The scenery began to change as we approached St Louis. We were now on the floodplain of the Mississippi River. Way off in the distance, the metal superstructure of a bridge glinted in the hazy sun, towering over the surrounding flatland. It was the biggest bridge I had ever seen. The approach road took us gradually higher and higher until the bridge came into full view. It was a breathtaking sight; we drove onto the narrow bridge with some trepidation, the wide and mighty Mississippi River flowed under the bridge a hundred feet below. The city of St Louis was now clearly visible on the Missouri side of the river. The bridge took us directly there, depositing our caravan into the noise and traffic of downtown St Louis. After an hour of complete disorientation, we found our way to Route 66 West.

We saw our first Stuckey's billboard shortly after getting onto Route 66. It advertised the world's best cherry cider, just a few miles ahead. The sign featured a tempting depiction of an icy mug brimming with cold cider. The billboard repeated every five miles or so. It was a sweltering afternoon, and we were still four hours from Joplin. A short time later, the distinctive Stuckey's facade came into view. Kenny turned into the parking lot; the others followed. Inside, each family bought a gallon of cider, pecan bars, and other assorted snacks. Mack and Stevie were disappointed to find Big Red soda was not available. In fact, the Stuckey's clerk had never heard of it before. We sat in a shaded outdoor gazebo and chugged three gallons of icy cherry cider. It was delicious, and so cold it made our teeth hurt. We were all young, and there were lots of things we still hadn't learned. Among the things none of us knew was the laxative properties of cherry cider. Cider was not a common drink where we came from. What little cider we did consume on the farm was made from apples. Most of the apple cider had been fermented into an alcoholic drink, and was consumed slowly, and in moderation. No one in their right mind would chug a gallon of the stuff, fermented or not.

We finished our rest stop, and pulled back onto Route 66 bound for Joplin. We brought up the rear this time behind Roy's Oldsmobile, with Bonny and Mack in the lead. We had only gone a short distance when Kenny and I became vaguely aware that something was not right. We exchanged puzzled glances as our discomfort grew. Audible bowel rumbles came next, followed by a sustained duet of high-pitched farts that set off peals of giggles from Stevie in the back seat. Up ahead, Mack in the lead car swerved into a Texaco gas station at a high rate of speed, and skidded to a stop. We followed Roy's Olds and crunched to a stop in the gravel parking lot next to them.

The vehicle doors flew open. The restrooms were twenty feet away; it was every man and woman for themselves. The Texaco station was out in the middle of nowhere, surrounded by trees. All three men displayed admirable chivalry and headed directly for the woods. I made a bee line for the Men's Room; Bonny claimed the Lady's Room. A desperate Evelyn, knees locked together, struggled to cross the gravel parking lot in her stilettos. She was forced to clamp and wait. Carl was relaxing in the Plymouth reading a comic book. He had given up the struggle back on the road, and dumped a load in his pants. Stevie and the little girls had not drunk the cider, and were spared. Back on the road, the giggles from the back seat resumed, causing Kenny and I to break into laughter too. Regardless of age, farts were funny, after all.

We approached the outskirts of Joplin after dark, and pulled into the first motor hotel we came across; we got adjacent cottages for the night, and turned in. The next morning, we were back on the road at sunrise. Nobody felt like breakfast; everyone was still queasy from the day before. Our destination today was Amarillo Texas. Soon after leaving Joplin, we crossed the border into Oklahoma. It was here that the scenery started to change. The forested rolling hills of Missouri gave way to flat plains and fields of crops. This is where I remember seeing the first Burma Shave signs. The shaving cream company posted witty public services messages on a series of signs as part of their advertising campaign.

Don't Pass Cars

On Curve Or Hill

If The Cops

Don't Get You

Morticians Will

Kenny and I looked forward to the Burma Shave signs, and slowed down a bit to read them when a new sign series appeared. We had a favorite:

Cautious Rider

To Her

Reckless Dear

Let's Have Less Bull

And Lots More Steer

The Will Rogers Turnpike was an early divided toll road with limited access. It started near the Missouri border and took us into Tulsa. From Tulsa, the Turner Turnpike took us the rest of the way to Oklahoma City. Aside from the Oklahoma turnpikes, Route 66 was a two lane road the whole way, from Illinois to California. It was just after leaving Oklahoma City that we saw our first sign for the Jackrabbit Trading Post near Joseph City, Arizona, eight hundred miles away. From here on, signs appeared with regularity, counting down the remaining distance to the curio superstore, and teasing motorists with promises of a Giant Jackrabbit outside for the kids.

Near the Texas border, the landscaped changed again. We were now driving across a vast prairie. The Texas Panhandle was flat as a pancake; prairie grass and grain crops waived in the stiff breeze as far as the eye could see. The sun was still high in the sky when we reached the Amarillo city limits. Everyone's appetites had returned full force. We stopped at a Phillips 66 gas station and questioned the uniformed attendant about local restaurants. He was nodding his head and smiling before Kenny finished the question. "Golden Light Cantina" was his immediate answer.

The guy at the gas station had it right; this was our kind of place. Bob Wills and his Texas Playboys played San Antonio Rose on the jukebox. Real cowboys sat here and there eyeing our entourage. The menu featured Texas size Burgers and beef brisket sandwiches, cold beer for the men, and lo and behold, Big Red soda. The owner even came to our table to sit and talk. It was he that told us the story of Big Red. The wonderful elixir had been invented in Waco Texas, and was the signature Texas soft drink statewide.

Big Red could only be had in two other states; Kentucky, where it was bottled in Louisville, and southern Indiana. We had a great time reliving the cider episode. The group was starting to bond as the trip brought us closer together. Even Evelyn was starting to grow on me.   The only thing I ever had against her was that she was gorgeous, and my husband wanted her.   Other than that, she was a real sweetheart.

 Mack had not taken part in our bubbly chat session; his attention was focused on two cowboys shooting pool and getting drunk few feet away. The path to the ladies room went by the pool table. The cowboys were amusing themselves by ogling and fake humping every lady that passed by on their way to the restroom. As soon as the restroom door closed, one or the other would place the pool cue between his legs and stroke it like a long skinny erection. They both put a finger down their throat and as if to induce vomiting when an older plus size lady passed.

Bonny and Evelyn got up to go to the restroom. Mack and Roy watched their wives squeeze by the pool table where the grinning cowboys waited. When the ladies had passed, the one nearest the restroom door extended his cue and mock goosed Evelyn. He sniffed the tip of the cue to the delight of his sidekick. Roy saw the whole thing, and rose to his feet.   Mack forcibly shoved Roy back into his chair, and strode to the pool table. Mack pulled a cue from the rack and broke it over the cowboy's head, then stepped forward, grabbed him by the hair, and slammed his head onto the slate pool table knocking him unconscious. Mack then went after his partner; he leaped over the pool table and grabbed the offender's sidekick by the throat. Now Roy was on the scene, trying to pull Mack away before he killed the guy. It took Kenny, Roy, and the cantina owner to wrestle Mack off of the terrified cowboy.

Bonny and Evelyn came out of the restroom with surprised expressions. They had no idea what had caused the carnage in the pool room. The cowboy on the floor was awake now, curled up in a ball, holding his head. Roy helped him to his feet and looked him over. The shock of Mack's sudden beating had rendered him sober, and contrite. Roy handed the cantina owner money to pay for the broken cue, and apologized on behalf of everyone for the ugly scene. The cowboys apologized to the ladies then we shook hands and were on our way to find a motor hotel for the night. Mack had not stuck around for the reconciliation; he had gone to the Plymouth where he sat in silence waiting for the others.

At sunrise we were on the road again, bound for Albuquerque. Kenny and I were still talking about the scene at the Golden Light Cantina, and what got into Mack. The scenery gradually changed from prairie, to a John Wayne western set. Shortly after crossing into New Mexico, a cloud of dust appeared on the road far ahead. A few minutes later we came upon the scene of an accident. A pickup truck towing a travel trailer had drifted onto the sandy shoulder, and rolled over several times. The trailer had split in half, and was blocking the road ahead. Shards of glass and clumps of insulating material were scattered all over the pavement. Several others had stopped; people were out of their cars, wandering around the wreckage in a daze. Mack had been leading our caravan. The Plymouth rolled to a stop in front of the wreckage; the doors flew open. Bonny and Mack jumped out and ran toward a twisted pile of debris. They were the first to see the two children who had been riding in the trailer. Mack lifted a piece of debris, Bonny reached into the crack and pulled out a young girl, injured, but very much alive. The girl's brother lay several feet away on the sandy shoulder. Mack kneeled next to the frightened boy and whispered assurances. Bonny carried his sister out of the wreckage, and placed her on the soft shoulder next to her brother. Bonny took complete charge of the scene.

The kid's parents had not fared so well. They were both alive, but unconscious. Kenny, Roy, and Evelyn, along with a half-dozen good Samaritans, had pulled them from the smashed cab of the truck, and were tending to them as best they could. I was sent back up the highway to warn approaching cars and was witness to one of God's daily little miracles: A man with a leather bag was running toward me. In the lineup of cars behind the wreck was a physician on vacation with his family. He came quickly to the scene, did a quick assessment of the injured parents then went to the shoulder where Bonny had triaged the children. The doctor introduced himself, and Bonny briefed him. She had bundled the kids when shock set in, determined no bones were broken, and monitored their vital signs as best she could. Mack had stayed beside the boy, who was conscious and crying out for his parents. He held the boy's hand and continued to assure him everything would be ok. One of the drivers who had stopped on the west side of the accident turned around and raced back to the nearby town of

Tucumcari for help. Everyone breathed a sigh of relief when we heard faint sirens and saw the distant flashing lights of ambulances coming from both directions.

With the family off to the hospital, we shook hands and hugged the others who also stopped to help. We huddled to compare notes before getting back in the cars; everyone was pretty shaken, and needed a timeout to regroup. A local among the good Samaritans gave us directions to his favorite watering hole in the town of Santa Rosa, an hour or so ahead on Route 66. We drove on, through Tucumcari, and arrived in the lovely little town of Santa Rosa in the late afternoon. We spotted the tall sign we were told to look for, and pulled in to the Club Café parking lot in time for happy hour. We washed up in the restroom then squeezed into a big Naugahyde booth with a round table. The men ordered two large pitchers of beer, and extra glasses to toast the hero of the day, Bonny. When the toast was done, we demanded to know her story, which was amazing and unexpected:

Bonny was in high school when the war broke out. She planned to leave the farm life but there was no money for college. In her senior year, a WAC officer came to the school recruiting for the Nursing Cadet Corps; the program offered free medical training in exchange for military service upon completion. There was a critical shortage of nurses in the early years of the war. Bonny was admitted to the program, and exceled in her studies. Her first assignment was at the Nissen-Hut Station Hospital in Somerset, England. It was here she met Mack an Army infantryman badly wounded a week after the Normandy Invasion. His unit had taken shelter in a barn. They were sound asleep when they came under fire from a German Panzer. The tank scored a direct hit; most of the unit died instantly. Mack suffered multiple shrapnel wounds to his back and legs, but survived to be evacuated back to England to start his long recovery. Mack still carried a shard of shrapnel in his lower back. He still had nightmares of the barn, and was sensitive to loud noises; he instinctively ducked whenever a car backfired or when a door slammed shut.

Once back on Route 66 bound for Albuquerque, Kenny and I yammered back and forth guiltily. We both had Bonny and Mack pegged as something akin to White Trash. How wrong we were. They had a remarkable life story, and were a living example of why you should never "judge a book by its cover." It was a beautiful drive through the Wild West landscape leading into Albuquerque. We arrived at the El Camino Motor Hotel and Dining Room on Fourth Street just after sunset. The day's activity, and the pitchers of beer, had taken a toll; everyone was exhausted. We said goodnight, and turned in. We had a long stretch ahead of us tomorrow; we were going to the Jackrabbit Trading Post, and overnighting in Winslow, Arizona.

10 THE WILD WEST

We left Albuquerque early the next morning. It was a beautiful crisp sunrise that showed the world in detail. We could see tiny little features on the mountain that rose abruptly behind the stumpy Albuquerque skyline. It was the biggest sky either of us had ever seen; crystal clear and blue, not a single puffy cloud. It was a wonderful morning and we were both in a great mood. I scooted over next to Kenny and put my head on his shoulder. Both of us were feeling amorous. On our last two nights in Indiana we had to sleep apart. Kenny and Stevie bedded down in the front room of Genevieve's house in Bethel Village. I got the trundle bed in my sister's sewing room. We had been on the road with no opportunities for days. Stevie was still in his pajamas asleep in the back, so we could speak freely for a while. Kenny said he was working on a plan to get a few hours alone at our next stop. I couldn't resist the opening to burn him with a question: "Why do we need a few hours when you never last more than five minutes?" Kenny responded with his Jackie Gleason imitation, wherein he sends Alice Kramden to the moon with a single punch. We were happy and playful, like two young river otters.

We reminisced about our carefree time in Fayetteville. I relived Mel's brilliant performance as the infected worm lady. Kenny was laughing hard; tears dribbled down his cheeks. I was concerned that he might lose control of the car and send us flying end over end through the rocks and cactus. I changed the subject to Rodney and Mary Mullis. By this time, they would have resumed the hillbilly life in their West Virginia hollow. Kenny painted the image of Rodney as Li'l

Abner running barefoot through a briar patch chasing supper. Mary, his Daisy Mae, would have lost most of her front teeth by now; the ones that remained stained brown from years of chewing Mail Pouch tobacco. Now we were laughing harder than before. I had always wondered, and had to ask: "When you guys got in trouble in Germany for moving the outhouse, did the fellow you were after really fall into the pit?" Kenny squeaked out a reply through his laughter: "Yes, Yes he did! And he had to get lotsa shots too." Now we were on the verge of wetting our pants. Stevie was up now, awakened by our hilarity.

Up ahead, we saw something fall from the undercarriage of Mack's Plymouth. We watched it spark on the pavement, and tumble along for a ways before bouncing off the road. The Plymouth was leaving a trail of fluid now. Kenny sped up and honked to get Mack's attention. Smoke billowed from beneath the station wagon as it coughed to a stop on the shoulder. We pulled up behind them and Roy followed. The men were all pretty knowledgeable about cars. They raised the hood, and crawled underneath to see where the fluid was coming from. Their unanimous conclusion was the old rusty station wagon was done for. We were joined by a State Trooper who radioed ahead to Holbrook for a tow truck. We had to make a new plan: Mack would stay and wait for the tow truck. The rest of us would drive on to Holbrook and secure a place for the night. Bonny and the twins rode in Roy's Olds, and Carl came with us.

I knew the awful story of Carl's life so far; Bonny had told me his story shortly after we met. I was glad to have some time with him. I got up on my knees and turned around in my seat to face the boys in the back seat. Carl's mother Joan was serving a prison sentence for second-degree murder.

Carl's father Mitch was an alcoholic. He was not a fun-loving drunk. He drank hard liquor every day and blamed everyone but himself for his miserable existence. Mitch became mean and violent when drunk; he regularly beat Joan with closed fists in front of Carl. One Friday night, there came a breaking point. Carl was awakened by a vicious late night fight. Carl came into the dining room to find his mother pinned to the floor, and his father holding a heavy rotary dial phone he had just ripped from the wall. Mitch was preparing to crush Joan's skull with the phone.

Carl charged him and jumped on his back, raining blows about his head with his little fists. Mitch turned on him in a rage. He grabbed Carl by the throat and punched him square in the face. He raised Carl up to eye level, then and flung him backwards into a china cabinet, breaking the glass doors and the cups and saucers within. The sound of breaking glass and Joan's screams snapped Mitch out of his drunken rage. Mitch grabbed his car keys and coat and left the house. He slammed the front door hard. The color JC Penny portrait of the smiling family flew off the wall near the door and shattered on the tile floor.

Miraculously, Carl was not badly hurt; he had one deep cut across his chest and several shallow cuts on his back from being flung into the china cabinet. Mitch's blow to Carl's face had knocked out a tooth, and cut both of his lips which were now swollen and discolored. Joan, herself bleeding from the beating she had received, tended to her son. She hummed *Amazing Grace* as she cleaned and bandaged his wounds and struggled to maintain her composure. Carl's heart was broken; he asked through his sobs if he had done anything wrong. He promised to never do it again.

Joan finished patching up Carl, then went next door to use the neighbor's phone. They were sound asleep; Joan pounded on the door. After a minute or two the door opened. The neighbors saw her injuries and immediately took her in. Joan called a cab, and went home to pack Carl's clothes and personal belongings. Joan arrived at sister Bonny's front door at daybreak. Mack took one look at the two, and went into his bedroom. He returned seconds later with his loaded .45 semi-automatic service pistol. Joan blocked his exit, and assured him she had the matter in hand. She asked that Carl be allowed to spend a few days with them while she and Mitch worked things out. Mack, still seething with anger, drove her home and offered again to take care of things his way.

Joan hugged her brother-in-law, thanked him again for taking Carl, and waved goodbye. Out back in Mitch's work shed was an unlocked wood cabinet. Inside there was a shotgun and a box of 12 gauge slugs used to hunt deer. Joan loaded a shell and went back to the house to wait for her husband. When the front door opened later in the morning, Joan shot Mitch in the face point blank. The slug struck his forehead, blowing away a circular piece of scalp that sailed gracefully back over the porch and onto the lawn. Bonny said that's all Joan remembers from that day: the top of Mitch's head spinning off and flying like a whirly bird, falling in a crimson heap on the wet grass twenty feet away.

I had seen postcards showing a hotel out west that had cottages built to look like Indian tipis. As we approached Holbrook, I saw what appeared to be a large Indian village in the distance. As we drew near, I realized it was the place on the postcard! The motor hotel was named Wigwam Village, and the Vacancy sign was lit; of course we had to spend the night. We checked in, got our tipis, and went into Holbrook to meet the tow truck bringing Mack and the Plymouth. They had arrived at the garage first. A mechanic there had looked the car over and determined the problem was fixable, but would take until the following afternoon to repair. That fit in nicely with our plans to cross the scorching desert that lay ahead at night. It also gave us a free morning to visit the Jackrabbit Trading Post a little ways further down the road.

The final road sign in the series that started in Oklahoma was a crude billboard announcing that you had finally arrived. The trading post building was long and low. To the left of the entrance sat a giant jackrabbit with a saddle and stirrups. Visitors could hoist their little ones aloft, and snap a photo of them riding the enormous bunny. Inside the door, we were greeted by the smell of leather. Narrow aisles ran here and there between racks of Wild West souvenirs and clothing. Stevie and Carl went straight for the toys: feathered tom toms, peace pipes, pop guns that shot a cork on a string, and bows that shot arrows tipped with sucker

cups. Glass cases on either side of the cash register
displayed hand-crafted Navajo jewelry made of turquois,
silver, and leather.   One glass case was dedicated to hand
carved Hopi Kachinas. There was a large selection of dolls,
and a thick pamphlet describing the meaning of each one to
the Hopis.

For tourists who wanted to learn more about the area and its
history there was a wall dedicated to reading material.
There were easy read books with color pictures of the Grand
Canyon, Meteor Crater, desert animals, birds, and reptiles,
and Hopi and Navajo customs. I found a rotating card rack
with the novelty postcards I loved: a cartoon cowboy leading
his horse home after a fishing trip, with a trout that looked to
be around 300 pounds tied to the side of the horse. On
another postcard, a nervous barber was shaving a bad
hombre with a six gun on his lap. On the wall behind the
barber's chair, the gunslinger's Dead or Alive wanted poster
was tacked to the barbershop wall. Next, I found the
postcard with a picture of Wigwam Village, the same one I
remember seeing in Indiana years earlier. I bought it, along
with a heart-shaped piece of petrified and polished wood
from the nearby Petrified Forest. Without thinking through
the consequences, we bought pop guns for the boys. A
short time later, we headed back to Holbrook to the sound of
uninterrupted popping corks and giggles.

Before air conditioned autos became the norm, summer
travelers on Route 66 timed their trips to cross the blazing
hot deserts of Arizona and California at night. We retrieved
the Plymouth from the garage and headed west out of
Holbrook in late afternoon. From here, Route 66 continued
west through Flagstaff and Williams. The road took us
through miles of pine forests before descending to Kingman,

and the low desert beyond. The men figured we would make Victorville on the west side of the desert by dawn the following day, allowing for one rest break along the way.

It was close to midnight when we crossed the Colorado River into California. It was one hundred degrees in the windy car, and dry as a bone. We pulled into a huge Texaco truck stop in Needles. We parked in a gravel parking lot full of idling diesel semis. We exited the cars and were hit in the face by a blast of hot wind and blowing sand that stung our eyes. Thousands of moths struggled in the wind around the lights above the gas pumps. We were all very tired and beginning to smell after being cooped up in our hot cars. We washed up in the restroom, and sat down for a midnight snack. The men huddled around a separate table and unfolded a roadmap to see where we stood; Roy announced we were on track, and would be through the worst of it by daybreak. We ordered our food, and sat in sleepy silence; the little ones in pajamas slumbered in the booth next to us.

An older, heavy set truck driver walked up to our table and introduced himself as Bud. He had noticed our Indiana license plates when we pulled into the parking lot. Bud was from Bloomington, Indiana, a town just thirty miles west of Columbus. He drove for Mayflower out of Indianapolis, and was bound for Tucson with a load of furniture he picked up in San Francisco. We invited him to sit with us. We shared stories about the Indiana homeland, and filled him in on our migration west. We told him San Diego was our planned destination, but at least one family would stay behind in Los Angeles. Bud had been to San Diego and Los Angeles on business for Mayflower. They paled in comparison, he said, to the city of San Francisco. Our food came; we ate our burgers and listened intently as Bud gave a glowing endorsement of the City by the Bay: The Golden Gate Bridge was breathtaking, Fisherman's Wharf had the freshest seafood, and there were too many great restaurants to count.

We left Needles bound for Barstow in the lead. Bud had made an impression on Kenny. He wondered aloud if San Diego was the right choice, and whether we should go to San Francisco instead. Bonny and Mack would be leaving us. They would settle down in Carson, a community in Los Angeles where the fledgling Wham-O toy company, Mack's new employer, was headquartered. Kenny and I both knew Roy would follow our lead, but Evelyn was already pressuring him to stay in Los Angeles; that's where Hollywood was, after all, and Bonny and Mack would be their neighbors. LA was also home to cutting edge hospitals and clinics that held hope for Lottie's diagnosis and treatment. So far this trip had been a team effort. Now we would be going it alone. Our spirit of adventure swelled, and we decided to push on to San Francisco, without Roy and Evelyn if need be.

At three in the morning, I lay my head against the side window. As the moonlit desert whizzed by, I was dreaming of the City by the Bay. Just then, a crackly, wavering broadcast from a station out of Salt Lake City broke through to the car radio playing Tony Bennett; it was a sign. Surely it was meant to be.

We arrived in Victorville just after sunrise; right on schedule. It was a beautiful high desert morning. A welcome chill in the air greeted us when we exited the car at Howard Johnsons for breakfast. We were all pretty beat, especially the men. They had been behind the wheel since leaving Holbrook the afternoon before with just the one rest stop in

Needles. Roy looked especially bad: He was pale, and even quieter than usual. Evelyn was noticeably concerned. Roy had complained of breathing problems in Barstow, and now she was softly insisting that he go to the closest hospital emergency room. Bonny went over and stood behind Roy's chair. She felt his forehead, took his pulse, and asked him a few questions. She looked up at Evelyn and calmly instructed her to call an ambulance; immediately.

Roy was transported to the Victorville medical center. Evelyn rode in the ambulance. Kenny and I followed. Bonny took Lottie with her twin girls, and Carl stayed with us. We sat in the hospital waiting room with the kids, waiting for word of Roy's condition. We were joined by a relieved Evelyn an hour or so later. Roy was stable and resting comfortably. Roy's ER doctor wanted to keep him overnight for observation. The nearest heart specialists were in Los Angeles. Evelyn was given a referral to a physician in Santa Monica, our destination at the end of Route 66. We all returned to the Howard Johnson and got rooms for the night. The adults were completely exhausted, and the kids getting cranky.

11 WELCOME TO CALIFORNIA

We met for breakfast in the Howard Johnson dining room. Evelyn had a quick cup of coffee then left in the Olds bound for the hospital. She was cute as ever, well-rested and upbeat. There had been no calls to her room during the night; a sign that Roy was recovering on schedule and all was well. This was an exciting day. We were one hundred miles, only two hours' drive, from road's end in Santa Monica. Sometime this afternoon, we would see the great Pacific Ocean for the first time.

We had a couple of hours to kill before Roy's release from the hospital. We found a grassy city park where the kids could run around and the adults could get some fresh air. We sat at a picnic bench and talked over what our next moves would be. We told Bonny and Mack about our new plans to settle in San Francisco. Mack was shaking his head *No* before we finished. He reminded us that the city had been destroyed by an earthquake fifty years earlier. It was common knowledge that another big one was sure to happen again. It could happen a hundred years from now, or it could happen tomorrow. In the Midwest, there were tornados outbreaks every spring. We had all grown up with the threat of being sucked up and killed by a funnel cloud. Mack could deal with that, but the thought of the earth moving under his feet terrified him. None of us had ever experienced an earthquake. That was about to change.

When we got to the hospital, Roy was getting a final exam before being discharged. We sat in the waiting room with Evelyn planning our day. With Roy in the clear, we could look forward to our final hours on the road. It had been an adventure, but we were all ready for it to be over. It was midday now; we were all hungry. I asked the discharge nurse who wheeled Roy into the waiting room for a recommendation. Without hesitation, she directed us to Emma Jean's hamburger place a few miles ahead on Route 66. We followed the others there. We waited at the cash register while tables were moved together for our party. Emma Jean's had a mascot; an ancient overweight Persian cat that sat on a carpeted perch in the foyer. Stevie and Carl delighted in scratching the old cat's chin and making it purr loudly. When we were seated, Roy was given the seat of honor at the head of the table. He looked to be his old self again. His color had returned, along with his smile and quiet sense of humor. We ordered the house special cheeseburgers and fries, and chattered excitedly about what lay ahead in Santa Monica.

I paused for a drink of water. Something odd caught my attention: The surface of the water in my glass roiled for no apparent reason. Dogs tethered in the yard behind the restaurant began barking hysterically. The Persian cat mascot in the foyer was going berserk. The whole building creaked, then shuddered, then started to shake. Then there was a sharp jolt; like the entire building had been lifted five feet in the air and dropped onto solid bedrock. Glasses, dishes, and silverware went flying. Some diners panicked, and ran for the front door of the restaurant, only to be knocked off their feet by the groundwaves that followed. I watched in disbelief as waves of energy raised and lowered the cement blocks that made up the walls of the building. The undulating blocks shattered the glass in the windows that looked out onto the highway. Power poles outside were swaying to and fro; the lines they held aloft danced like skip ropes. Here and there outside, clouds of dust rose up from

the high desert where something had fallen. The rolling
shake went on. The crashing sound of breaking dishes
came from the kitchen, followed by a loud electrical pop that
knocked out the lights. Then it was over. We sat in the dark
in shocked silence. I heard the distant cries of a terrified
child, shoes crunching on broken glass, and the sound of
running water from a broken pipe. A moment later, a chorus
of distant sirens came from the direction of Victorville. The
earthquake that seemed to go on forever had lasted less
than a minute from beginning to end. It was the longest
minute of my life so far. We found Mack under the table
curled up in the fetal position, Bonny kneeling beside him,
tenderly squeezing his hand and whispering assurances.
The jolt had snapped Mack back in time to the Normandy
barn; to the moment the Panzer shell blew his platoon to
pieces.

The boys were shaken, but unhurt. At the outset, Roy and
Evelyn had instinctively grabbed for the twins who sat
between them in high chairs. Roy now held the twins, one
on each arm, while Bonny worked to calm Mack under the
table. Kenny and I took Lottie in her carrier and went to the
front of the restaurant to see how the others had fared.
Several diners were tending to an older gentleman on the
ground near the front door. He had been knocked to the
ground and landed on a shard of window glass. He had a
nasty gash on his forehead that was bleeding profusely.
Everyone else appeared to be okay. A dozen or so diners
and restaurant workers had fled the building, and were now
walking around the parking lot in a daze.

We went back to our table to see how Mack was doing. He
was up sitting in a chair, being loved on by Bonny and
Evelyn. We brought the news that everyone in the building

had escaped injury except the old man. Bonny left her husband in our care, and went with Kenny to see if she could help. The cook had just arrived with a First Aid Kit from the kitchen. Bonny elbowed her way to the old man's side, and politely ordered the others to stand back. She took charge of the scene, just like she had done at the trailer accident. Bonny chatted with the old fellow as she worked, telling him he was going to be fine, but probably not able to go out dancing come Saturday. She sanitized the wound, and wrapped gauze about his head to hold the sterile pad firmly in place. The old geezer looked like a mummy when she was done. In the distance one of the faint sirens was drawing near. A moment later an ambulance pulled into the parking lot. Mack had regained his composure; his terror now turning to embarrassment. Bonny got behind the wheel of the Plymouth to spell Mack for the drive to San Bernardino.

We pulled out of the restaurant parking lot in the lead. We turned on the radio for news of the earthquake. We learned that the epicenter was 120 miles away, at a place called Wheeler Ridge in Kern County. The quake measured 7.3 on the Richter scale the announcer said, and was the strongest ever to hit Kern County. Twelve people had died closer to the epicenter in buildings that didn't withstand the jolt and shaking that followed. Kenny and I were beginning to reevaluate our plans to settle in San Francisco, a city that sat astride the biggest known earthquake fault in California. San Diego was starting to sound pretty good again to both of us.

We were overjoyed to finally see the Mojave Desert slipping behind us in the rearview mirror. A wall of mountains now rose in front of us. On the other side was Southern

California. We were climbing now to go through the mountain wall at Cajon Pass. Out of my passenger window, I was watching a freight train struggle up the grade at ten miles an hour. The train appeared to be miles long. I couldn't see where it began or where it ended. From Cajon Pass, Route 66 descended into the town of San Bernardino. We led the others into a Phillips 66 station on the outskirts of town to stretch, and fill up.

Everyone was starving. Our order of cheeseburgers and fries had died on the grill when the earthquake hit. We had all gotten by on crackers and chips we had in the car for Mack and the kids. There was a restaurant less than a half hour away in Rancho Cucamonga that Evelyn had heard of. It was a favorite of celebrities traveling between Palm Springs and Los Angeles. It sounded inviting, but I worried that such a place was probably a bit too pricy for our ragtag group. Roy, generous gentleman to the end, sealed the deal by offering to pick up the entire tab. "Well, all right then!" I blurted out. I was starving. The thought of a juicy steak made my mouth water. Evelyn was all a twitter at the prospect of catching a glimpse of a celebrity. It would be a grand celebration of our safe arrival in Southern California.

One of Evelyn's Hollywood magazines had done a special piece on The Sycamore Inn and Steak House. She rummaged through the trunk of the Oldsmobile and found the article. She gave it to me to read on our half hour drive to Rancho Cucamonga. The place had a long history. It derived its name from the dense gallery of sycamores and cottonwoods that once grew along a live stream flowing out of the ten thousand foot San Gabriel Mountains that formed a towering backdrop to Rancho Cucamonga. The original Inn was built in 1848. It had been a stop on the old

Butterfield Stage Line. After a succession of owners and enterprises, it became a favorite watering hole for travelers on the main artery between Los Angeles and points east.

We pulled into the Sycamore Steak House parking lot at high noon. The front of the building was rather unimpressive. The inside was dark with lots of polished wood and dark burgundy Naugahyde chairs and booths. Framed, autographed photos of *A List* celebrities lined the forest green walls above the vertical oak wainscoting. We were seated around a heavy wooden banquet table with linen napkins and a full complement of silverware. We ordered a round of steaks for the adults and cheeseburgers with onion rings for the kids. This was a real treat. Beef had not been a big part of our Indiana farm diet. What little beef we did consume was usually made part of a hearty stew. We toasted our safe arrival in Southern California; I said a brief prayer of thanks, and we dug in. My steak was tender and delicious; the best I'd ever had by far. Evelyn finished her meal quickly then embarked on a self-guided tour of the autographed celebrity photos.

Evelyn was gone for quite a while. I was getting ready to go looking for her when she appeared, grinning ear to ear, with a handsome older gentleman. She introduced him as Jack Bailey, assuming the rest of us also knew who he was. We all politely looked up from our plates and feigned excitement at meeting the stranger. Mr. Bailey pulled three business cards from his jacket pocket and handed one to each of the ladies. He invited us to come to Hollywood and be in his studio audience for a future show. Mr. Bailey shook hands with the men then promptly excused himself. The business card identified the stranger as Jack Bailey, the host of a local television show called *Queen for a Day*.

The highway west out of Rancho Cucamonga took us through mile after mile of fragrant orange groves. It was paradise compared to the arid deserts we had just spent days to get across. The landscape was green again. Not near as green as Indiana, but pleasing to the eye just the same. We were nearing the coast now. Outside air temperature was steadily dropping from the low nineties when we left Rancho Cucamonga, to a perfect seventy-five as we neared Santa Monica. We could see the city skyline of downtown Los Angeles off to the south now. The endless miles of citrus groves were now giving way to residential neighborhoods of tile-roofed Spanish homes, and craftsman bungalows. We saw the blue horizon of the Pacific Ocean for the first time as we descended into Santa Monica.

Route 66, the Mother Road, ended unceremoniously at the intersection of Olympic and Lincoln. We drove a couple of blocks further west looking for a suitable rest stop. We found a palm lined parking lot atop a bluff overlooking the Pacific Ocean, and parked. It was a clear, blue summer evening without a breath of wind. The glassy surface of the ocean sparkled. Waves crashed onto the beach below the bluff where we sat. Sunbathers were packing their towels and coolers as the sun sank low in the sky. The high pitched squeals of kids playing in the surf rose above the roar of breaking waves. To the south of us, a wide pier extended out beyond the breaker line. There was an amusement park there. We heard a strange mix of calliope music from the distant pier, and a chorus of ukuleles from a luau party on the beach in front of us. Our ragged band of weary travelers sat here and there on the grass at the edge of the bluff taking it all in. We sat in silence, alone in our individual thoughts. The last thousand miles of our eventful trip through scorching wasteland had taken a toll on all of us.

We lay strewn about on the grass like marathon runners who'd just crossed the finish line.

We sat there in blissful silence until the sun disappeared into the sea. Bonny and Mack had a place to stay the night. They gathered up the twins and left for nearby Carson where Mack's brother was expecting them. Carl stayed behind with us to be with Stevie; they had become good buddies. Kenny and Roy left in the Oldsmobile to secure rooms for the night. They were back in a jiffy, excited about their find. We had ocean front rooms on the beach just two blocks from the bluff where we sat. We would be there two nights, after which we would part and go our separate ways. After we had checked in and unpacked, Evelyn and I sat on the boardwalk seawall outside our front door. We hatched a plan for a farewell beach party the following night. They would be staying in LA at least at first. Roy had a referral to a heart specialist in Santa Monica. Roy planned to ask the specialist for a referral to a pediatric internist for little Lottie. Bonny and Mack planned to settle in Carson near his brother. Mack was scheduled to start his new job immediately. Kenny and I were still bound for San Francisco on our own.

12 THE END OF THE ROAD

I woke up to the pleasant sound of breaking waves just after sunrise. I met Evelyn on the seawall for morning coffee. It was a brilliant sunny day. A warm wind blew from the east, sending veils of spray off the wave crests. Roy was getting dressed for his appointment with the heart specialist. Evelyn and Lottie were going too, leaving me and Kenny to begin preparations for tonight's farewell beach party. Mack was getting a tour of the Wham-O factory where he would be working. While the men were off taking care of business, Bonny's sister-in-law was taking her on a house hunting tour through LA's residential neighborhoods. They would join us in the evening for the beach party.

When Kenny was up and about, we sketched out a shopping list and set off to buy the party supplies. We left Stevie and Carl to play on the beach in front of our cottage. We hadn't filled the Chevy since our gas stop in San Bernardino. We rolled into a Pacific Highway Texaco station running on fumes. In those days, men with hats and crisp uniforms took care of everything; they came running to serve you; checked your fluid levels, pumped your gas, and washed your windows. I went inside the station looking for the Coke machine. I was still getting used to the fact that there was no Big Red to be had in the entire State of California. I pulled a cold bottle of Royal Crown Cola from the cooler. I returned to the car to find Kenny chatting with the uniformed attendants. The Texaco crew had us topped off and ready to go. Kenny drove to the far edge of the gas station property overlooking the ocean. He turned off the motor and we just sat there in silence, drinking it all in. We were here.

We did it together. We left everyone we knew and gambled on an uncertain future. We were a team working for a common goal; our bond had never been stronger.

There was a tap on Kenny's window. It was a uniformed Texaco attendant wanting to say something. He had come across the parking lot to give us a message. Kenny rolled down his window. The man handed Kenny a rolled up newspaper; "You left this in the station" he said, then smiled and walked away. Kenny sat still for a moment in a way that told me something about the brief encounter had shaken him. I asked if there was a problem; he said it was nothing. We didn't recognize the attendant as one of the team that had serviced our Chevy. The oval patch on his uniform identified him as *Marty*. Neither of us had bought a newspaper; he probably had mistaken us for the other young couple we had seen fueling up at the same time. Kenny shrugged, and tossed the newspaper into the back seat.

We returned to our beach cottage in the afternoon. The trunk of the Chevy was loaded with beach party supplies: soda, chips, beer, hotdogs, and two bundles of firewood. Stevie and Carl had spent the day splashing in the surf, and building stuff out of wet sand. Their alabaster Indiana skin was a dreadful shade of red; they were terribly sunburned from a full day under the July sun. Another lesson learned. There was a concrete fire ring directly in front of our cottage, just a hundred feet or so from the water's edge. Carl and Stevie helped Kenny lug the firewood and other stuff to the fire ring and get it set up. Bonny and Mack arrived with the twins just before sunset. Mack took over as Grill Master. He took several wire coat hangers from the cottage closet and fashioned them into weenie roasters. He took the family cooler from the Plymouth and loaded the beer, soda, hotdogs and ice, from the trunk of the Chevy. With Kenny's help, the heavy cooler was muscled across the sand and positioned upwind of the fire ring where Mack planned to set up shop. Roy and Evelyn arrived after sundown; they looked tired and careworn from their day of medical appointments. Kenny met Roy on the boardwalk and handed him a cold can of beer; he guzzled it without stopping to breathe. Roy took a second beer and chugged it in the same manner. Feeling renewed, Roy took Lottie in her carrier to the fire ring where Bonny and I were getting a rundown on the day's events from Evelyn.

The men were starting to get looped. Mack was in rare form; it was nice to see him laugh and smile for a change. He had fashioned a gas station street map of LA into a ridiculous looking chef's hat. He was busy loading up the coat hanger roasters with weenies and handing them out to the rest of us. Mack wore Bermuda shorts and went shirtless; shiny ridges of scar tissue crisscrossed his lower back where shell fragments from the Panzer round had ripped into him. Mack laid out hotdog buns and condiments on top of the cooler then picked up his daughters, one in each arm. He rocked the girls to and fro singing *Hey Good Lookin'* until they were sound asleep. Mack quietly returned them to their blanket, covered them up, and opened another beer.

Kenny and Roy were getting pretty lit up too; they had been engaged in a private reminiscence of the Cherry Street Grocery days. They were laughing out loud. Among their regular customers were a handful of rude malcontents capable of ruining an otherwise pleasant day at work. Kenny taught Roy the art of sidestepping anger, and getting even instead. This was a Phillips gift. It didn't take long before Roy no longer dreaded the approach of a foul curmudgeon, but actually looked forward to it; to seeing what kind of diabolical revenge Kenny had cooked up for the unsuspecting grouch. Roy was too nice, if that's possible. Kenny was the perfect partner for Roy, and they had come to be very fond of each other. Mack felt the same way about Roy, and he and Kenny gladly assumed the role of enforcer to protect their friend from anyone who would take advantage of his kindness.

We finished our burnt weenie feast, and sat in silence around the fire. My attention was drawn to Bonny. She sat on a beach towel on the other side of the fire, lost in her thoughts. The flickering light from the bonfire brought into sharp relief the worry lines carved into her noble face by life's trials. She sat on her towel with her long legs crossed. Bonny was the second tallest of our group after Roy, high waisted and slender. I felt a head on my shoulder; it was Carl. I had been wrong in my initial assessment of all of our fellow travelers; this was especially true with Carl. The dirty little urchin I first saw in Columbus was in truth a sweet, sensitive child. Carl had been subjected to horrors no adult should have to endure, let alone a young boy. Now there was another head on my other shoulder; it was Stevie. To my eternal regret, he too had been witness to the ugliness of family violence. I squeezed them both and said a silent prayer of thanks and contrition. The sunburned boys looked like little lobsters; they were both in for a day of pain tomorrow. The long day had taken the starch out of them; soon they were collapsed against me, sleeping soundly.

It was close to midnight when we put the last log on the fire. It was time to pack up and head back to the cottages. The men's beer buzz had peaked, and they now turned their attention to lugging coolers, blankets, and kids back across the sand to the boardwalk. Bonny and Mack were headed back to Carson for the night taking the twins; Carl stayed with us. I bedded the boys down on the front porch where the cool sea breeze would lessen their discomfort. After the kids were put down for the night, Kenny and I met Roy and Evelyn on the seawall for a night cap. They filled us in on the results of their earlier medical appointment: the heart specialist was satisfied with Roy's vital signs and overall condition. The doctor's attention quickly turned to Lottie who Evelyn had brought to the examining room.

The doctor excused himself, and returned five minutes later with a pediatric oncologist who had a practice in the same building. The pediatrician asked Evelyn several questions then examined Lottie. Her symptoms were indicative of childhood leukemia. The doctor offered a ray of hope; San Diego was the site of groundbreaking research into childhood leukemia; a new Children's Hospital was under construction there. He gave Roy and Evelyn a referral to a San Diego pediatrician specializing in childhood cancers; they would be leaving for San Diego in the morning. Roy and Evelyn were not shocked by the doctor's grim conclusion. They had known in their hearts for months that their daughter was gravely ill. We hugged and said goodnight at two in the morning. We returned to our cottages to get some sleep; tomorrow our caravan family would be parting for the last time.

My internal alarm clock was still set to farm time. I was wide awake at sunrise; never mind I had only gone to bed four hours ago. I felt like company, so I pestered Kenny until he gave in and got dressed. There was a morning coffee place by the pier just a short ways up the boardwalk. We tiptoed past Stevie and Carl on the porch and went for coffee.

Kenny stopped by the Chevy and grabbed the newspaper the Texaco guy had brought us the day before. After a short walk we arrived at an outdoor patio that sat atop a bluff by the pier. We chose a table with a great view of the ocean and coastline. Kenny went to the window for two coffees while I split up the newspaper: sports page and classifieds for Kenny and the rest for me. The newspaper was a San Diego Tribune with a banner headline that jumped off the page at me: "Ryan Aeronautical Lands X-13 Contract" it said. The article that followed explained that the X-13 was an experimental jet fighter that could take off and land vertically; no need for an airstrip. The project would require Ryan to hire several hundred new manufacturing positions. Apprenticeships were available and veterans had preference for all training programs.

Kenny returned with our coffees. I tossed him the front page and sipped my coffee while he read. Ryan Aeronautical, Kenny recalled, was the company the sailor spoke of in the Cherry Street Grocery that blustery day last February. We talked about it: neither one of us was really happy about taking off to San Francisco alone; we had both felt a nagging sense of uncertainty that we hadn't shared until now. The starting salary for an apprentice machinist at Ryan would be double the money Kenny earned working as a grocer in Columbus. It was an easy decision; made easier knowing that Roy and Evelyn would now be our neighbors in San Diego.

We needed to top off the Chevy before leaving Santa Monica later in the day. I wanted to take that opportunity to thank Marty at the Texaco station for his consequential mistake. San Diego was only two hours' drive south of LA; we would enjoy tonight's sunset from our new hometown.

Kenny went to find the Men's room. I picked up the San Diego Tribune front page to read the Ryan article again. I noticed something strange for the first time: The paper was dated March 26; it was now early July. The newspaper Marty brought to us was over three months old. Kenny returned and we started down the boardwalk to our cottage. Now I wanted more than ever to talk to Marty at the Texaco station.

Bonny and Mack were at the cottage when we got back. Bonny was tending to Stevie and Carl on the front porch. Their shoulders were nearly blistered from a full day exposed to the July sun; both boys were in a great deal of pain. Bonny had picked up a first aid cream from a drugstore on the drive over from Carson; she was gently rubbing the soothing mixture onto the boys' burned skin. Roy and Evelyn were up and about. Mack and Roy were sitting on the seawall making plans for a fishing trip as soon as the families got settled in. Evelyn was helping Bonny doctor the boys. We announced to the group that we had decided to go to San Diego. Kenny joined the fish planning session on the seawall to the delight of Mack and Roy. The twins needed to be changed and bathed. I took Bonny's place alongside Evelyn and finished medicating Carl and Stevie, who were beginning to enjoy the effects of the soothing lotion.

We checked out of our cottages just before noon, and gathered in the parking lot to say goodbye. Roy and Evelyn had already made an appointment with the San Diego pediatrician who would see Lottie. They had to be in the doctor's office early the following morning to get the process started. They had made arrangements to stay the night at a hotel near the clinic. The Oldsmobile was the first to leave the parking lot; Roy waved and hit the "La Cucaracha" horn. Roy and Kenny had made plans to get our families together in San Diego in a month. Bonny and Mack had found a rental near Carson. They planned to stay with Mack's brother until the first of August when the unit would be ready.

After a round of handshakes and hugs, we left in different directions. Our first stop would be the Santa Monica Texaco station to top off the Chevy. We got to the station and drove to the lookout point at the far edge of the station parking lot. It was a glorious clear sunny day. The ocean was calm and glassy. The clear air gave us a real sense of how huge the view was before us. Large fishing boats appeared as little white specks on the blue water. The outline of Catalina Island rose from the horizon twenty-six miles away. In the vast sweep of sea, a massive naval aircraft carrier near the horizon looked like a child's bathtub toy.

We drove across the parking lot to the Texaco station. Kenny stopped at the pumps and got out. He was met by a team of uniformed Texaco attendants. Kenny asked the guy who appeared to be in charge; "Is Marty working today?" The guy said he didn't have a Marty on his shift, but suggested he talk to the station owner. Kenny went inside, and located the station owner in a grimy office at the far end of the service bay. Kenny returned to the car a few minutes later with a blank expression on his face; no one named Marty had ever worked at the Texaco station during the five years since the station commenced operation in 1947.

We left Santa Monica and found southbound Highway 101 to San Diego. I yammered away about the mysterious Marty. My theory was that the uniform Marty wore looked remarkably similar to a Texaco uniform, but was not: Marty could have been a mail carrier, security guard, milk man, or any other uniformed worker who saw the newspaper in the station and thought it was ours. That made perfect sense to me. I had no explanation for the San Diego paper. It was months old, and the timely front page article changed the direction of our lives. In the end I chalked it up to coincidence and dumb luck; it was something God apparently wanted us to see and that was His way of putting it in front of us. Kenny listened to my evolving theories without comment. He was unusually quiet, causing me to ask if something was the matter. He said it was nothing. That meant to me that it *was* something; something Kenny didn't want to talk about yet.

13 OCEAN BEACH

The sailor who visited the Cherry Street Grocery on that
fateful day in February had spoken fondly about Ocean
Beach, a San Diego beach town on the Pacific Ocean just
west of downtown. He had a favorite place to stay on his
visits to Ocean Beach; it left an impression on Kenny. The
sailor had described an ocean front hotel consisting of a
cluster of cottages built on pilings. In the center of the
cluster of cottages was a viewing hole with a railing around
it. At high tide, waves washed through the pilings and could
be seen as the white water passed over the sand beach at
the bottom of the hole, illuminated by colored floodlights.
The hotel was called the Ocean Village; Kenny had taken
notes and knew the way there.

The two hour drive to San Diego on Highway 101 took us
through a series of charming little beach towns. The road
hugged the coast nearly the whole way, with beautiful
coastal vistas of empty white sand beaches and breaking
surf. We exited Highway 101 in San Diego at Harbor Drive,
and followed the signs west to Point Loma, and Ocean
Beach. Harbor Drive ran east-west along the northern shore
of San Diego Bay. Naval vessels on mooring buoys sat in a
long line in the middle of the channel. A seaplane landing
strip defined by a long string of lighted buoys ran parallel to
the roadway just offshore. On the opposite side of Harbor
Drive we saw the main runway for Lindbergh Field, San
Diego's airport. We crossed a small bridge and passed a
sign announcing the community of Point Loma.

We followed signs showing the way to Cabrillo National Monument at the tip of Point Loma. The meandering route took us up a canyon to an intersection at the top of the grade. Catalina Boulevard ran along the narrow spine of the peninsula and dead ended at the lighthouse. We turned left on Catalina and drove the four miles or so to the Park Service parking lot at end of the road. The lighthouse sat on a high point hundreds of feet above the surrounding ocean. The view was stunning: several islands were clearly visible on the southern horizon; rugged mountains framed the downtown San Diego skyline far off to the east. To the south and west, the sea went forever in all directions; I was still marveling at the vastness of the Pacific Ocean.

Kenny dug through his wallet and located the crumpled piece of paper with the Ocean Village information he had scribbled down months earlier. We backtracked down Catalina Boulevard to the intersection with the canyon road. This time we turned left on a street that descended to sea level on the windward side of the peninsula; it was appropriately named Hill Street. The bottom pitch of Hill Street was extremely steep. Our view of the vast Pacific changed quickly as we descended; as if we were in a glass elevator. A cross street intersected Hill at the bottom. There, on the southeast corner of the intersection, sat an empty duplex with a for rent sign in the window.

Kenny stopped and I went across the street to jot down the information on the sign: two bedroom duplex, unfurnished, available immediately, fifteen dollars a month. Not more than a hundred yards away, sheer sea cliffs dropped straight into the ocean; I could hear the muffled roar of waves crashing into the base of the cliffs. The duplex was on the northern edge of a large housing complex. The sign identified the former military housing project as Azure Vista.

The road into Ocean Beach ran along the top of the sea cliffs a ways before entering a neighborhood of modest homes similar to those I had seen in Santa Monica: wooden craftsman style bungalows and white stucco Spanish style homes with red tile roofs. We took a left onto Newport Avenue, the central business district of Ocean Beach. All of the average family's daily needs were there: a bank, two drug stores, two grocery stores, department stores for men's and women's clothing, a medical building with doctor's offices, and an assortment of beer bars and restaurants. Ocean Beach Elementary School sat at the east end of the Newport business district; at the west end, Newport Avenue took a hard right at a low seawall. Beyond the seawall a wide sandy beach stretched northward for a half mile or so.

We found the Ocean Village Hotel at the north end of Ocean Beach. To Kenny's dismay, the place turned out to be an utter dump. Years of thrashing by storm waves, and perpetual dampness, had taken a toll on the former vacation destination. We parked and got out to have a closer look. A boardwalk led across the sand and up a short set of stairs into the cluster of dilapidated cottages. We found the railed balcony overlooking the open hole to the beach below. It was low tide. Stevie excitedly pointed to something moving on the sand below. Several black rats were fighting over an odiferous dead sea creature. Cockroaches scampered here and there on the moldy cottage walls. I had noticed a hotel on Newport Avenue that looked quite nice. We returned to downtown Ocean Beach and got a room for the week. We ate a meat loaf and mash potato supper at the Village Townhouse restaurant, just a block up the street from the hotel. Kenny would go to Azure Vista in the morning and see about renting the duplex. I was concerned about the danger to Stevie; a fall from the nearby cliffs would almost certainly be fatal. Other than that serious concern, we were both pretty excited at the prospect of living right on the sea for fifteen dollars a month.

The Ocean Village Hotel

The next morning Kenny left in the Chevy for Azure Vista. When he was finished there, he planned to go back over the hill to Harbor Drive, to the Ryan personnel office. We had passed the Ryan buildings yesterday on our drive past Lindbergh Field. I took Stevie and walked to the Ocean Beach Elementary admissions office to inquire about school. I mentioned we were looking into renting a place at Azure Vista, which I learned had its own elementary school where Stevie would need to be enrolled. I found a phone booth outside a Newport grocery store, and placed a collect call to Florence in Indianapolis. Long distance phone calls in those days were very expensive. I kept it short and sweet: we were safe at our destination, and we loved our new home by the sea; details would follow in the mail.

That afternoon I sat on the hotel's shaded front porch writing letters home. Stevie had a little patch of grass to run around on, and an unplanted flower bed of dirt to dig in. A couple of older ladies passing by on the sidewalk stopped to chat and make over Stevie. They introduced themselves as Pat and Leila. I gave them a brief recap of our caravan adventure, and told them it was our family's first full day in town. The ladies and their husbands had also relocated from the rural Midwest together. They had settled in Ocean Beach in the 1930's. *OB*, as they called it for short, had become their beloved forever home; a paradise with healthy fresh salt air, an ocean on one side, and a beautiful bay on the other. Crime was non-existent, and many young families like ours were moving to the neighborhood. The ladies suggested I bring the family for a service and social at their church some Sunday. They were members of the Ocean Beach Baptist congregation, which was growing by leaps and bounds due to the influx of young families. I thought it sounded like a great idea; a place to meet other couples with kids, and start making new friends. I thanked them for the invitation, and assured them we would come as soon as we got settled in.

Kenny pulled up in front of the hotel in the late afternoon grinning ear to ear; he brought nothing but good news. He had secured the duplex at Azure Vista, and paid the first month's rent plus a small deposit; we had the keys, and the green light to move in. We had four nights left at the hotel; plenty of time to round up some basic furniture. The duplex came with a stove and refrigerator, so all we really needed were two beds, a kitchen table and chairs, and a few things to sit on for the living room. Kenny saved the best news for last; he had been hired on the spot for a machinist trainee position at Ryan. He had to report the following morning for a physical exam, and bring his discharge papers to verify his status as a veteran. We celebrated the day's blessings with a meal of comfort food from the Village Townhouse restaurant, followed by a walk on the beach. The sunset that evening was appropriately beautiful. OB was already starting to feel like home. A week later we moved into our new home on Hill Street.

The duplex was small. We had a tiny kitchen with a window above the sink that looked out over the ocean. The living room was the only large room in the house. We set up our new kitchen table and chairs in the corner nearest the kitchen and made it into a family dining area. Our bedroom was quite small; Stevie's was even smaller, but adequate. We had one bathroom with a tub and shower combination, commode, and sink. Outside, we had a private patio and unpaved parking spaces for two cars. It was August now, and very warm. We slept with the windows pushed open and doors unlocked. A latched screen door let in the cool sea breeze and kept the bugs out. I loved falling asleep to the sound of breaking waves. No two nights were the same. When the ocean was flat it was quiet, but that never lasted more than a day or two. I got the best sleep of my life on Hill Street.

The day we parted company with Roy and Evelyn, the men set a date in August to rendezvous and catch up. We didn't have phones so there had been no communication for a month. Not knowing where anything was in San Diego, the men unfolded a San Diego street map and noticed a pier extending into the sea in Pacific Beach where Roy planned to settle. They agreed to meet at the base of the pier at high noon on Saturday August ninth. The day finally came; I was looking forward to seeing our friends. The drive to Pacific Beach only took twenty minutes or so. We found Garnet Avenue, the main drag. Garnet dead ended at the ocean where we found Crystal Pier and Roy and Evelyn waiting for us. We hugged each other up then took a table at a nearby outdoor bar on the boardwalk.

Evelyn brought both bad news and great news; Lottie's initial diagnosis of childhood leukemia had been confirmed, but now there was hope. She was being treated by one of the world's leading authorities on the disease. There had already been dramatic changes for the better. I peeked into her carrier; the little girl looked back at me with sparkling eyes for the first time. She was smiling and curious about the world around her. Roy and Evelyn had rented a mobile home at De Anza Cove, a trailer park on the shores of Mission Bay. There was a sand beach right outside their front door for swimming and fishing. Evelyn proposed we get together for a beach weenie roast the following night. Roy had inherited a heavy saltwater rod and reel from the previous tenant, along with a steel toolbox full of hooks and sinkers.

The next day was Sunday. We had plans to visit the OB Baptist Church for the morning service and social, but had no plans after that. We agreed on an late evening beach party; eating hotdogs and potato salad, swimming in the warm bay, and fishing with Roy's newly inherited outfit. Kenny told our friends the story of Ocean Beach, and finding a house on the ocean in Azure Vista. Evelyn and I exchanged addresses and determined who would bring what for tomorrow's party. We sat on the seawall next to Crystal Pier and watched the sun sink into the sea, then went our separate ways.

We arrived at the OB Baptist Church the following morning looking snazzy; Stevie wore his long sleeve white dress shirt with a black bowtie and suspenders, I was decked out in my best dress with gloves, and matching hat and purse; Kenny

looked handsome and dapper in his coat and tie. My
favorite part of worship services was the singing of hymns.
The Baptist hymnal was nearly identical to the one we sang
from at Columbus Methodist. We stood and sang together:
*The Old Rugged Cross, This is my Father's World, Amazing
Grace, and I Come to the Garden Alone.* The sermon was
inspiring, and blessedly short. After the service, we mingled
outside on the lawn socializing with the congregation. Leila,
one of the ladies I had talked to from the porch of the
Newport Hotel came over with her husband for a formal
introduction. They were John and Leila Petty, a couple close
to our parents' age. Mrs. Petty invited us to their home for
dinner the following Saturday; we gladly accepted. Thus
began a friendship that would be an important part of our
early life in Ocean Beach. Kenny and I officially became
members of the OB Baptist congregation two weeks later.

That evening we arrived at De Anza Cove and found the
address Evelyn had given me. Their new home was a single
wide house trailer that was small, but neat as a pin. We
found Roy sitting in a chair under the trailer's awning sipping
a beer. Just across the road was a white sand beach. Roy
and Evelyn had everything set up for the beach party: the
cooler full of food and beer sat atop a new folding table
along with a Coleman lantern; two bundles of fire wood were
stacked and ready to go. At the water's edge Roy's big rod
and reel rested in a pole holder he had fashioned out of a
section of pipe from under the trailer. A pound of frozen
squid lay thawing on a cutting board next to the pole holder.
The locals at the bait shop told Roy what to do: bait a whole
squid on a big hook, cast it into the bay as far as you can
throw, then wait.

Kenny and Roy had done a lot of fishing back home. They knew how to catch Bass and Bluegill. The biggest sport fish in the Midwest was the Catfish. Both men had caught channel cats several pounds in size. Now they were about to get in over their heads; they had no idea what they were doing in this new salty environment. Evelyn and I were in for an evening of slapstick comedy. The show started at sunset, after several hotdogs and beers.

At the bait shop Roy learned that the rod he inherited was a homemade Calcutta; a ten foot piece of bamboo with line guides wrapped on with thread and adhesive. A conventional Penn reel attached to the Calcutta with two automobile hose clamps. Roy picked out the biggest hook in the toolbox and baited it with a huge squid. Kenny insisted that he was the more experienced fisherman of the two, and should make the first cast: he got into position, cocked the big pole back, and let the squid fly. The bait slammed into the bay a few feet away; the spool on the reel kept running, creating a huge mess of knotted line called a backlash, or *Birds Nest* in the fishing world. Kenny made a clumsy effort to put the Calcutta back into the pipe rod holder but failed. Roy's Penn reel fell into the dry sand sending grit into the gears and making the knotted line more difficult to work with.

The men plopped down under the Coleman lantern and began the arduous task of untangling the mess. Neither spoke, indicating things had gotten a little tense after Kenny's screw ups. After a half hour of patient picking, the outfit was ready for another try. Roy threaded another huge squid on the hook, and landed a good cast with minimal backlash. Roy set the clicker on the reel so we would know if a fish ran with the bait. Another round of beers helped restore joviality to the scene as we sat and waited for a bite.

It didn't take long. In the dim lantern light, we watched the big Calcutta rod suddenly bend then stand straight up again. Just as Kenny and Roy rose to their feet, the rod buckled and the reel clicker screamed as line raced off the spool. Roy pulled the rod from its holder, and hung on. Line was racing off the reel at a worrisome rate; the spool was coming into view, and they were powerless to stop it. Just then, the fish changed direction and headed up the beach toward the mouth of the inlet that led to the sea.

I grabbed the lantern and Stevie; Evelyn picked up Lottie in her carrier, and we followed the men up the beach as they fought the fish. Roy was able to gain some line back as they walked up the beach; he handed the outfit to Kenny who continued to put line back on the reel. Stevie was given a turn; Roy stood behind holding onto his belt loops to keep him from being pulled into the bay. The heavy Calcutta outfit was hard for Stevie to handle; after a few exciting minutes, he was ready to give it up. Roy took over just as the fish changed directions and headed back down the beach in the opposite direction.   By the time the fish was brought into view, we were back at the fire ring where we had started.

None of us was ready for what we were about to see. The fish was worn out and stationary in the dark water just off the beach; its exhausted movements roiled a big patch of surface water marking its location. Kenny rolled up his pant legs and waded in with the lantern while Roy tended the pole. When the water reached knee deep Kenny held the lantern high over his head. He peered into the deeper water in front of him, and saw the creature for the first time. I asked him what he was seeing; "Holy Shit!" was his answer. Kenny waded back to the beach. He described the thing he saw as a fish with wings and no fins and a long tail. He and

Roy worked together to gently pull the beast into shallow water. Kenny took a deep breath, waded in, grabbed it by the top of the head, and dragged it onto the sand. It didn't look anything like any fish I had ever seen; it looked more like an alien from outer space. It emitted deep guttural sounds, as though it was trying to talk to us. Kenny estimated the weight to be at least a hundred pounds. It looked to be five feet from wing tip to wing tip and had a long rat-like tail. It was covered in slime and didn't have any scales. Kenny's hands were covered with smelly goo from touching the head. Roy rummaged in the toolbox and found a pair of needle nose pliers. He removed the hook and dragged the creature back into the water. The fish sat quietly in the shallows for a few minutes regaining its strength. The shallow water exploded when it finally jetted away.

The locals at the bait store told Roy the fish was a Bat ray, and they were year round residents of Mission Bay. They reached a weight of two hundred pounds and were harmless if you avoided a stinger near the base of the tail.

Bat Ray

We got back to Azure Vista at two in the morning. A full moon was setting over the sea creating a narrow shining path of shimmering light on the surface. Stevie was sound asleep. Kenny carried him from the Chevy to his bedroom and tucked him in. Stevie was getting big now; it wouldn't be long before we could no longer pick him up. Kenny and I went out on the patio to have some alone time.

It was very still; the sea was flat and quiet. From our seat on the patio we could see the shining path from the setting full moon stretching from the horizon to the base of the cliffs. I had some news for Kenny; I was pregnant again. It hadn't been confirmed by a doctor, but I knew. I had been throwing up every morning since we moved to Azure Vista. We had always planned on having another child; we were hoping it would be a girl this time. The news perked Kenny up. He was surprised and delighted, and waxed smarmy at the thought of a little red-headed girl to be a little sister to Stevie.

Stevie on Sunset Cliffs near Osprey Street 1954

14 LETTERS FROM LUSCOMBS

Stevie started the second grade at Azure Vista Elementary in September. The school occupied a corner lot three blocks south of our duplex. The ocean view from Stevie's classroom was spectacular. The playground was situated right on the cliffs, on the other side of an alley that ran behind the school buildings. Balls accidently kicked or thrown out of the school yard during recess were lost to the sea.

A new elementary school was under construction at the top of Hill Street to replace Azure Vista which was scheduled to be closed and demolished. I got in the habit of taking an afternoon walk to the school to meet Stevie then go to a place I found on the cliffs to write letters home. At the end of Hill Street a sandstone point extended a several hundred yards into the sea. There was a field of boulders where I had found a comfortable place to write while Stevie played. I chatted with the young men with surfboards who stopped near the boulders to apply paraffin wax before going into the water. I learned the local folks referred to the point and surf break as "Luscombs." It became my favorite place to hang out and write letters home.

I began saving my incoming letters to read at my special place in the Luscombs boulder field. One day in late October a letter arrived from Genevieve in Columbus. She brought the sad news that our precious Uncle Charlie had passed away at the Greensburg Odd Fellows Home the week before. His funeral had already taken place in Madison, where Uncle Charlie was laid to rest. I shed a few quiet tears, but knew it was for the best; his health had continued to decline since I last saw him before leaving Indiana. He was free now and, I prayed, in a better place. I was concerned about Daddy and how he was holding up. Mom had written a month earlier about the passing of Delbert Phyfer, Dad's brother in law and fellow Main Street loafer. Daddy and Delbert had grown very close; they shared a bawdy sense of humor and the burden of being scorned by their mutual mother in law, Emma Humphrey.

A letter arrived from Bonny. We had been out of touch for over three months. They had bought a new home in Redondo Beach, only two blocks from the ocean. Mack loved his new job helping to ready the Hula Hoop for production. Making the hoops out of wood proved not to be cost effective. Mack was helping design the production tooling for making the hoops out of plastic instead. His brother had made him a limited partner in the fledgling toy company, so if the simple gadget was successful Mack stood to make a lot of money. It would be hitting the market soon and they were excited to see if anyone would buy it.

Bonny was working part time as a hospital emergency room nurse. Monday through Friday, she handed off the twins to Mack and left to work the evening shift in ER. Bonny still had the *Queen for a Day* business card from our run in with Jack Bailey. She proposed that we set aside a day in the future to go see the show. I thought it sounded like a fun time; Bonny volunteered to make all the arrangements. Carl's mother Joan was scheduled to be released from prison in January, and would be coming to Redondo Beach to live with them. Carl was doing well in school, and looking forward to being with his mother again.

I had written big sister Florence regularly since we left Indiana. I kept her updated on our adventures on the road, and our new life in San Diego. Florence was there the day Stevie was born. She had special feelings for her nephew and was missing both of us terribly. I was overjoyed when a letter arrived from Indianapolis with the news that Florence and Ernie were coming to California to see us. Ernie had just returned from Detroit with a brand new Buick Roadmaster and was itching for a road trip. They would be leaving in the spring when the weather improved; about five months from now.

The San Diego weather turned cold and rainy in late November, putting an end to our outdoor afternoons at Luscombs. In February Donna Kay, our redheaded baby girl, was born at Quintard Hospital in San Diego; the family's first native Californian. Our little duplex would be adequate for a while, but we would eventually need a bigger place. The Azure Vista complex would be demolished in two years and the ocean view lots sold to builders. All the other homes in the neighborhood were owner occupied and not available as rentals.

It would take a few more years of saving before we could buy a home of our own. Ocean Beach had a variety of properties for rent, so we began looking there on weekends for a full size house. We were driving around north Ocean Beach on a Sunday after church and came across a house on Voltaire Street with a sign in the front yard. We stopped and got out to read the sign; the house would be available soon and the price was right. It was a cute Craftsman style bungalow with a white picket fence around the front yard, and a huge backyard with fruit trees. It would take longer than expected, but the house on Voltaire eventually became our next home.

Baby Donna Kay Phillips February 1954

In May we took a short vacation to visit Bonny and Mack. Kenny had earned a week of leave from Ryan by that time. I was eager to show off Donna Kay, and the men were looking forward to finally fishing together. Bonny, true to her word, got us into the *Queen for a Day* studio audience for a live show. Mack and Kenny were going deep sea fishing on a boat out of Redondo Beach; Joan would watch over the kids for the day.

The day finally came to attend *Queen for a Day*. Things took an unexpected turn when I was chosen from the studio audience to be a contestant on that day's show. I was competing against two other women. We were instructed to tell the audience what we wished for most, but could not afford. The audience would then judge the stories, and decide who would be *Queen for a Day* and have their wish come true. I was caught completely unprepared: The only thing I could come up with was money to build a road from the Cook farm to Main Street in Paris Crossing. My parents were aging, and increasingly unable to safely walk the railroad tracks to get to and from home. My wish lost out to another contestant who stole the show: Her late husband was a cop. He had been shot and killed recently in the line of duty, leaving her widowed with four young children and a meager survivor's benefit; she just wanted money for a proper headstone for her husband, and new school clothes and shoes for her kids. The sob story had the audience and host Jack Bailey in tears, and won her the crown and bouquet that came along with being named *Queen for a Day*.

We headed home from Redondo Beach with a cooler full of fish fillets and my game show consolation prize: an enormous box of laundry detergent, and a new steam iron. It was May nineteenth; my birthday. We got home to Ocean Beach and found two cardboard boxes on the front porch that had just been delivered. The first box was from Columbus; it was very heavy. The box contained birthday cards from my sisters, and a case of Big Red soda; exactly what I was hoping for. The smaller box was from Mom and Dad Phillips. It contained more cards, an embroidered scarf made by Cammie, and a nostalgic six pack of Blatz beer for Kenny sent by his brother Charles.

Kenny had picked up a bag of charcoal and our first hibachi grill in Redondo Beach. A deckhand on the sport fishing boat had given Kenny and Mack a tutorial on how to properly prepare the Yellowtail fish that made up most of the catch that day. Soon we were relaxing in the patio listening to the fillets sizzle on the grill, sipping Blatz beer and Big Red, and enjoying the kids. It was a warm, blissful evening in Ocean Beach; a fitting end to a wonderful birthday, and the promise that next year would be the best year yet.

I spent a lot of time thinking about Marty, the Santa Monica Texaco mystery man whose dated newspaper had changed the course of our lives. I had heard stories from the Indiana elders that told of accident scenes where a person with grievous injuries was saved by a stranger who was never seen again. In other stories, a strange person showed up just in the nick of time to save the day, then disappeared without a trace.

Many of the elders were of the belief that there were angels among us who sometimes appear in human form. I had also wondered for a long time about the unnamed sailor who happened into Roy and Kenny's store and changed the destiny of three families: as a result of that brief encounter, Roy and Evelyn's daughter was saved from a tragic early death. Lottie was now a happy little girl with sparkling eyes and the hope of an eventual cure. Bonny and Mack had gotten a much deserved break that they sorely needed at that exact moment in time. Gone forever was the hardscrabble life in Columbus; eking out a living in a busted trailer with its trashy surroundings. They now lived in a snug Spanish home in a nice neighborhood close to the ocean in Redondo Beach. It had a granny flat in back where Joan and Carl now lived.

For Kenny and I, the move brought us closer together and put our rocky marriage on a solid foundation. So maybe the sailor and the Texaco guy were angels; guardrails on the curvy road of life. Or maybe it was fanciful thinking born from a need to believe in something bigger.

Everything Kenny had experienced in life so far, regardless of how weird it seemed, had turned out to have a logical explanation. I had the experience of the cemetery bunny and Grandma's steamer trunk to open my mind to another dimension beyond what we know as everyday reality. Kenny's first peek into *the world beyond* came the moment he made eye contact with Marty; it took Kenny a long time to open up about it. Kenny had recognized the Santa Monica Texaco man as the sailor who had come into the Cherry Street Grocery back in February. Marty didn't look like the sailor, and didn't talk like the sailor, but some sense deep inside Kenny *knew* he was the same person; the same life force. He was startled and frightened; he thought he might be losing his mind.

His fear was multiplied by the strangeness of the dated San Diego newspaper and its consequential headline. Now Kenny had to resolve the issue internally for his own peace of mind. He happily accepted my plausible explanation; it put his mind to rest once and for all:

Marty was a uniformed worker from another nearby business who mistakenly brought us the paper thinking it was ours. The dated San Diego Tribune paper with its timely front page article was just a fortunate coincidence. As far as thinking the sailor and Texaco man were one in the same, it was a mistaken impulse brought on by too much sun and beer. Of course I knew better.

EPILOGUE

Mack made a small fortune from the Hula Hoop craze. He bought a sprawling ranch home in Palos Verdes Estates with room for Joan and Carl. The twins, now five, attended their first year of school there. Bonny and I kept in touch for a few years, but no longer had much in common and eventually quit communicating.

Joan took to spending the summer days on the beach at Palos Verdes Cove. It was there she met a surfer her age from Manhattan Beach who took a shine to Carl and volunteered to teach him how to surf. The surfing lessons at the Cove blossomed into a storybook romance for Joan, who later remarried and moved to Manhattan Beach. Her new husband adopted Carl, who had a real dad for the first time in his life. Father and son took every opportunity to surf together at the local breaks.

Kenny and I continued to socialize with Roy and Evelyn. There were many more beach parties and Bat rays.   Little Lottie was able to live a normal life until the leukemia returned and overtook her. Lottie passed away a week shy of her fifth birthday. Evelyn was devastated and went into a deep depression. Roy had more than he could handle with Evelyn's breakdown, and his own health problems. They made the decision to move back to Indiana; to the love and comfort of their extended families. As with Bonny, Evelyn and I kept in touch for a while but eventually drifted apart.

I took to Ocean Beach and the beach culture naturally. Stevie began surfing at an early age and made lifelong friends who shared his passion for the sea. As soon as Donna Kay was old enough I enrolled her in the Ocean Beach School of Dance where she excelled. We became members of the growing Ocean Beach Baptist family, many of whom were our age with young children.

There were rough times ahead for Kenny and I; many of the little problems of old started to resurface as bigger problems. The church was a blessed oasis where, once a week, I could commune with the Lord and gather my strength for the week ahead. I had a deep faith rooted in first-hand knowledge of the comforter, the Holy Spirit. In the dark years that came next, when I was at the end of my rope, the comforter came to save me. After all of the words in my prayers were exhausted, the Holy Spirit came. It wasn't mysterious like a floaty ghost, it was familiar and simple; a river of pure Love for Me that brought instant peace and tears of gratitude.

BETTY LOU

Made in the USA
San Bernardino, CA
24 April 2019